16 Octr, 1863

The
Ancestors and Descendants
of
RULEF SCHENCK

A GENEALOGY OF THE ONONDAGA COUNTY, NEW YORK, BRANCH OF THE SCHENCK FAMILY

———

BY

BENJAMIN ROBINSON SCHENCK, M. D.

FROM

RECORDS AND NOTES
COMPILED

BY

ADRIAN ADELBERT SCHENCK

———

DETROIT, MICHIGAN
1911

THE WILSON PRINTING COMPANY
DETROIT, MICHIGAN

ADRIAN ADELBERT SCHENCK
1842-1909

THIS BOOK IS PUBLISHED

IN

MEMORY OF

ADRIAN ADELBERT SCHENCK

WHO DEVOTED MANY OF THE LEISURE HOURS
OF A BUSY LIFE TO COLLECTING THE
FACTS HEREIN RECORDED

PREFACE.

For many years my beloved father, Adrian Adelbert Schenck, cherished the ambition of putting on record the genealogy of that branch of the Schenck family which originally resided in or near Onondaga County, New York. The exigencies of an active business life left him but little time for working upon the thousands of details of a book of this kind, yet as opportunity offered, he corresponded with those from whom information could be obtained and carefully recorded names and dates, with that wonderful patience which was such a predominant trait of his character. One who has not tried to gather together facts about which there are no books and no authorities, little realizes the difficulties which beset such work. Letters are carelessly answered or are entirely ignored, records are imperfect as to full names and complete dates, and the memory often fails at a critical point. Unless one has the time to work continuously at such a task, it progresses but slowly and it therefore took many years for my father to collect the facts here recorded.

After the death of my father, which occurred February 25, 1909, I found a large number of letters, written records and newspaper clippings, which he had gathered and which he had just begun to arrange in chronological order for publication. It has required some time to complete the information and put it in form for the printer. My thanks are due to a number of cousins who have willingly and enthusiastically supplied missing names and dates. I am especially indebted to Mr. James Shuler Schenck for his energetic aid. Nearly all of the latter part of the book has been submitted in manuscript form to some member of the various families for inspection and correction, and no little trouble has been taken to have the records complete and correct. It can hardly be hoped, however, that there are no errors; for such as may occur, I ask the indulgence of the reader.

For many of the facts in the early history of the family in America, we are greatly indebted to the late Rev. Garret C. Schenck of Marlborough, New Jersey, who spent upwards of fifty years in the preparation of a complete genealogy of the Schenck family. This, however, has never been published. In 1883, father spent some time in New Jersey, looking up the records of the second, third, fourth and fifth generations in America, and I know that he was greatly aided by the Rev. Mr. Schenck. We owe much also to the records of Lieut. A. D. Schenck, U. S. A., whose book, *Rev. William Schenck, His Ancestry and Descendants,* has supplied me with many valuable facts. The connection between the Rev. William Schenck and the Ohio branch of the family on the one hand and Rulef Schenck and the Onondaga branch on the other is recorded on page 60.

The genealogy in Holland was compiled by Jonkheer William Frederic George Louis van der Dussen, Knight of the Order of the Oak Crown, Lieutenant Colonel and Commandant in 1873, of the Fortress of Nimeguen. He was editor of a genealogical journal at the Hague and one of the genealogical authorities of Holland. His work, formerly in the possession of Rev. Garret C. Schenck, is an immense volume, handsomely bound and clasped.

In 1885, there appeared a twenty-six page pamphlet entitled *The Blyenbeck and Afferden Branch of the Family of Schenck van Nydeck*. This was reprinted from a work, *The Family of Schenck van Nydeggen,* which was published in Cologne, Germany, in 1860. From this pamphlet I have obtained many of the facts contained in the first part of this book.

In 1876, P. L. Schenck, M. D., of Flatbush, L. I., published *A Memoir of Johannes Schenck,* the progenitor of the Bushwick branch of the family. This has been of great help in elucidating a number of important points in the early American history of the family. There are many descendants of Johannes Schenck and their relationship to our branch of the family is clearly shown on page 60.

The present book has been prepared primarily to serve as a record for those descendants of Rulef Schenck who are now living. The arrangement and method of numbering are modifications of those recommended by the New England Genealogical Society. It will be readily understood, yet a word of explanation on the significance of the numbers and the use of Roman numerals may not be out of place. The genealogy is in three parts:—
(1) From the year 1346 to 1650, where the unbroken line of descent is traced from Heinrich Schenck van

Nydeck to Roelof Martense Schenck, who was the first of the name in America; (2) from 1650 to 1776, in which section the American ancestry of Rulef Schenck is given; (3) from 1776 down to the present day, where may be found the descendants of Rulef Schenck in all the collateral branches. In section one (Part II.) the name of each individual mentioned is preceded by an Arabic numeral followed by a capital A. This is the key number. The Roman numeral preceding a name signifies the individual's place among the brothers and sisters of the immediate family, i. e., whether first, second, fifth or sixth, etc., child. The Roman numeral following the name signifies the generation. To avoid confusion the generations in Part III. date back to Roelof Martense Schenck, that is, they refer only to the generations in America. Roelof Martense represented the ninth generation from Heinrich. In some of the families among the descendants there are now children of the eleventh generation in America. They can therefore trace their ancestry back through twenty generations, or approximately five hundred years. In section two of Part II., from Roelof to Rulef, covering five generations, the key number before the name of each individual is followed by a lower case a, thus 12a. In Part III., the key number stands alone. Whenever an individual is mentioned the name is followed by the key number, thus avoiding the possibility of any confusion on account of similarity in names. Each individual who has married is carried forward into the next generation, a reference being given to the page. By the use of the key numbers, it is very easy to trace back a line of descent.

This book is published and distributed as a memorial to Adrian Adelbert Schenck, who died February 25, 1909. He believed, as did the children of Israel, that each generation should leave to posterity its own record and that these records should be carefully preserved. It was his expectation and hope that when his book should appear, it would be carefully preserved for the children and the children's children of all who received a copy. Care has, therefore, been taken to select a paper which will endure and an ink which will not fade.

The editorial work has not been done so well as would have been the case had he who first planned the book been graciously spared to have completed it, yet it is his spirit which permeates it and the credit for whatever of merit it possesses belongs to him.

B. R. S.

Detroit, Mich., June 1, 1911.

SCHENCK—In Syracuse Thursday, February 25, 1909, of angina pectoris, Adrian A. Schenck, aged 67 years. Funeral services were held at his late home in Syracuse Sunday. Mr. Schenck was born in Plainville but has lived in Syracuse since 1862. He is survived by his wife, one son, Dr. Robert Schenck of Detroit, and one daughter. Robinson

TABLE OF CONTENTS

PART I

	Page
Coat of Arms - - -	13
Derivation of the Name -	14
Holland History -	17
Early American History - -	27

PART II

The Holland Ancestry of Rulef Schenck	55
The American Ancestry of Rulef Schenck	61

PART III

The Descendants of Rulef Schenck	65
Seventh Generation in America -	66
Eighth Generation in America	80
Ninth Generation in America - -	100
Tenth Generation in America	126
Index - -	133

PART I.

COAT OF ARMS.

Seipmacher is the authority quoted by A. D. Schenck for the arms and crest of the van Nydeck branch of the family. In the language of heraldry the description is as follows:—

Arms—Sable, a lion rampant, or., langued et armè. Gu and az.

Crest—Out of a coronet, or., a demi-lion rampant, or., langued et armè. Gu and az.

In explanation it may be said that it was the custom among the knights of the middle ages to display their armorial ensigns, or arms, upon their shields and banners, and their crest, or cognizance, also worn by their followers, upon their helmets. When not engaged in battle, a coat of light material was worn over the steel armor and on this was worked, in colors, the arms and crest. This is the origin of the term coat-of-arms, a translation of the French, *cotte d'armes.*

A "coat-of-arms," as we use the term to-day, consists of two parts:—(1) The arms, displayed usually on a shield or banner, and above this, (2) the crest, usually resting on a crown in the case of a sovereign family or on a coronet, in the case of families of lower rank.

By referring to the colored frontispiece, the description of the arms and crest, as given above, will be understood.

On the sable (black) banner is a lion rampant (charging). This is painted in gold (or). The lion's tongue is protruding (langued) and he shows his talons (armè). The tongue is red (gu.) and the talons blue (az.)

The crest represents a demi-lion or half lion, similar to the lion of the arms, charging out of a coronet.

DERIVATION OF THE NAME.

The family names of all the countries of Europe are derived from one of five sources, and it is possible to trace every surname to one or another of these five divisions, which are:—

1. Baptismal or personal names, such as Thompson, Williamson or Richardson. As Bardsley says, it is easy to see how they came into existence, for nothing could be more natural than that children should often pass in the community as the son of Thomas, or the son of William, or the son of Richard. In some particular generation the sobriquet became permanent and passed on to future generations as an hereditary surname.

2. Local surnames, such as Lane, Styles, or Wood have survived from such designations as John of the Lane, William atte Style, or John atte Wood. There are many instances of this source in every language.

3. Official surnames have been bequeathed to us by the dignitaries of mediaeval times. Examples are Mayor, Baron and Bishop.

4. Surnames of occupation are very numerous, as a moment's thought will readily convince one.

5. Sobriquet or nicknames form a large class. Applied originally to individuals on account, perhaps, of certain personal characteristics they at some period became hereditary and survive today.

In attempting to classify a given name in any one of these divisions, however, it must not be forgotten that many names, especially in America, are not what they seem, but are in some instances corruptions and in other cases translations.

The name Schenck undoubtedly belongs to the third class, that of official surnames. The name signifies cup bearer and is derived from the same root as the German verb *schenken,* meaning "to pour out." Lieutenant A. D. Schenck in his *Rev. William Schenck, His Ancestry and Descendants,* explains the origin of the word.

The oldest term designating the office of cup-bearer, is *Skinker,* of Sanskrit origin. A more recent origin is possible, however, as it may be connected with either of the Anglo Saxon words *scaene,* a cup, or *scanca,* a shank. The first of these derivations is easily understood, the second requires an explanation. It has been supposed that the shank bone of an ox was used as a spout for a leathern wine bag. This use of a bone is said to be the origin of the cups of the butlers of England, the little knobs on the covers representing the shank-bone spouts of ancient times.

Whatever may be the origin of the word, it is common in several European languages, thus in Icelandic, *skenka,* in Danish, *skencke,* in Dutch and German, *schenk,* and in French, *eschanson.*

Several of our ancestors are referred to as *Pincerna.* This is the Latin translation of the same word. Thus the first of the Van Nydeck branch of the family is referred to as *Christianus Pincerna.* He was cup bearer to the Count van Julich, whose residence was the famous castle of Nydeggen. There are records of Julich in which he speaks of *Pincerna noster* (our cup bearer). All legal documents of this time (1225) are in Latin and this form of the name, *Pincerna,* appears in them. In "low" Latin, the name became *buticularius, bucellarius, busellarius,* and similar words, all denoting the "leather bag man." From these is derived the French *bouteiller,* and the English *butler.*

Cup bearers were probably employed long before history takes notice of them. We know that among the ancient Kings of Media the cup bearer held the first rank in the royal household. He had charge of the household arrangements and was the King's chief attendant when at home, guarding him from interruptions when engaged, and acting, in fact, as master of ceremonies. Both in ancient and mediaeval times, it was one of the duties of this officer to taste the wine before it was served. This was done by pouring some into the palm of the hand and was to guard against the possibility of poisoning the master. The office was always held by a noble and in feudal times became hereditary.

Thus it was that many noble families, in the middle ages, bore the name of Schenck. There are sixty-eight families of the name mentioned in the *Kueschke Deutches Adels-Lexicon*.

HOLLAND HISTORY.

The Holland ancestry of Rulef Schenck may be traced in an unbroken line to the year 1346. At this time the head of the family was the Knight Heinrich Schenck van Nydeck, Lord of Afferden and Walbeck, from whom the line of descent, as given later (Part II.), has been recorded by van der Dussen, formerly one of the most noted genealogical authorities in Holland, who searched long and patiently to complete the work. While there are breaks in the record previous to 1346, we are fortunate in possessing not a little information concerning the family as early as the year 878.

Before relating these facts, however, it may be of interest to briefly sketch, in outline, the history of the Netherlands and attempt to form some conception of the character of its people.

The Netherlands, or nether lands, was the name given to the countries situated in the small triangle between the France and Germany of today and the sea, the territory which is now about equally divided between the modern countries of Holland and Belgium. It was a country traversed by overflowing rivers, harassed by the sea and devoid of beauty. Of its earliest inhabitants we know little, for history records nothing previous to the epoch of Julius Caesar. The wars waged by the conqueror, rescued from oblivion the Celtic and German tribes, whom he found in this hollow land, or Holland, and Tacitus, the Roman historian, has minutely described their characteristics. Motley, whose *Rise of the Dutch Republic, The United Netherlands* and *John of Barneveld* will long remain the authorities on early Holland history, thus translates and embellishes the more prosaic paragraphs of the Latin:—

"Physically the two races resembled each other. Both were of vast stature and the gigantic Gaul derided the Roman soldiers as a band of pigmies. Both were fair, with fierce blue eyes, and clear blonde complexions. Their hands and feet were small. The especial mark of high rank was the brightness of the eye, and long hair was considered beautiful. They were races remarkable for personal dignity, which early became corrupted into excessive pride, and for a boundless spirit of individual enterprise. With these traits, they united a simplicity and truthfulness, which was always observed by strangers. They were notoriously reckless of their own lives and cruel to enemies; fond of the chase and of adventure, especially on the sea, preferring whatever involved peril and hardships; greedy for booty and given to the pleasures of the table and to gaming."

The government of the tribes differed somewhat, yet with all of them, it was essentially republican. Clanship was a predominant feature. The Gauls were an agricultural people, while the Germans were more given to war and carnage. The Gauls were priest ridden and their Druids were a predominant class. The German tribes, however, held to a simpler faith, believing in a single, supreme, almighty God.

First conquered by Caesar, these truculent tribes, despite many revolts, several unsuccessful confederacies and numerous rebellions, remained subject to Roman rule for about five centuries. With the decline of the Empire, the Netherlands were "successively or simultaneously trampled by Franks, Vandals, Alani, Suevi, Saxons, Fresians and Sclavonians, as the great march of Germany to universal empire went majestically forward."

The Frank dominion succeeded the Roman and the history of the Franks became the history of the Netherlands. Against this dominion struggled through several centuries, the Fresians, who held the northern part of the territory, until finally conquered by Charlemagne in 785. That great emperor, however, was succeeded by unworthy and incapable men who had not the sense to comprehend, far less to develop, the plans of their ancestor. Charles the Simple was the last of the Franks to govern Lotharingia, in which was comprised most of the Netherlands and Freisland, and the sovereignty, in 925, passed to Henry the Fowler. Thus, the Netherlands passed out of France into Germany, remaining still provinces of a loose, disjointed empire. At this period the various petty earldoms, dukedoms, etc., became hereditary. Sovereign counts became numerous and autocratic, and the force of arms became dominant.

"Five centuries of isolation succeeded. In the Netherlands, as throughout Europe, a thousand obscure and slender rills were slowly preparing the great stream of universal culture. Five dismal centuries of feudalism, during which period there is little talk of human right, little obedience to divine reason. Rights there were none; only forces."

Out of the chaos of these dark ages gradually evolved a people, three million strong, whom Motley in his enthusiasm, calls "the most industrious, the most prosperous and perhaps the most intelligent under the sun." The Hollanders of the sixteenth century were unequalled as agriculturists, as merchants, as mariners, and as artisans. Their natural industry was untiring; their prosperity unexampled; their love of liberty indomitable; their pugnacity proverbial. "Within the little circle which inclosed the seventeen provinces were two hundred and eight walled cities, many of them the most stately in Christendom, one hundred and fifty chartered towns, sixty-three hundred villages with their watch towers and steeples, besides numerous other more insignificant hamlets; the whole guarded by a belt of sixty fortresses of surpassing strength."

Such, very briefly, is the history of the Netherlands— a mere outline serving to show inadequately the characteristics of the people among whom were our ancestors. The reader who is interested, will find a lengthy and most picturesque account in the historical works of Motley, to which reference has been made and from which I have freely quoted.

The first information which we have of the Schenck family concerns Colve de Witte, Baron van Toutenburg, who was killed in the battle of Clodius against the Dane in 878. The records of the successors to this title and barony are imperfect, but, according to A. D. Schenck, sufficient have escaped destruction in the wars of the middle and succeeding ages, to establish the fact that the same family held possession down to, and even much later than, the year 1234 when one of the cadets became the first of the family of Schenck van Nydeck.

Following Colve de Witte, there is a record of:—

Hermanus Schenck, Baron van Toutenburg. Then:—

Willem, who perished at the first tournament held in Germany, at Magdeburg in 939. He was followed by

Hermanus II., in turn succeeded by

Willaim, who is recorded as taking part in the seventh tournament, held at Halle, by the Emperor Henricus II., in 1042. The next record concerns

Reynier Schenck, Baron van Toutenburg, who had three sons, Theodorus, Christianus and Albertus.

Theodorus Schenck, the eldest son, became the next Baron van Toutenburg. There was a succession of Barons in this family, through seventeen generations, down to Joost, or George, who in 1521 was Governor of Friesland, Groningen and Overyssel. His son, Fredericus, the last Archbishop of Utrecht, noted for his learning and many literary productions, died August 25, 1580. This branch of the family became extinct in the twentieth generation, when an only son, Jacob, died when a child.

The second son of Reynier, Christianus Schenck, became attached to the retinue of Count van Julich, whose residence was the famous castle of Nydeggen. He was

called Christianus Pincerna and his name is to be found
as witness to various documents of Julich between 1225
and 1246. He held the important office of cup bearer
to the Count. It may be said, in explanation, that the
cup bearer of these times was the head of the household,
the protector and confidant of his chief and the master
of ceremonies at the court. Christianus was apparently
held in high esteem by the Count, who in a document
of 1234 affectionately mentions him as Pincerna noster
(our cup bearer). On September 10, 1250, he was
appointed, together with Marschall van Kelser and Renad
van Druse, a court of justice to settle a dispute between
the Count and Conrad van Hochsteden, Archbishop of
Cologne. In some of the documents he is spoken of as
Christianus Pincerna de Nidke, the Dutch form of which
is Christianus Schenck van Nydeck. His coat of arms,
as given by Seipmacher, forms the frontispiece of this
book. Christianus had one son,

Wilhelmus, whose name appears in 1275 and 1287
as witness, and in 1275 as a court of justice in a dispute
between the monastery at Kerpen and the Lord of the
castle. On April 1, 1279, he and his four sons sold to
the church syndicate of Cologne all their estates in Geyen,
namely, "one manses cultivated land, the decram of every-
thing raised thereon and their rights and privileges of
patrons of the church of Geyen." Wilhelmus' wife died
in 1271 and was buried in the New Cloister, Graevendael, near Goch. In her memory Wilhelmus presented
to the convent an annual revenue; the document, bearing
the date of March 13, 1271, tied with red silk threads

and sealed with green wax, being now in the archives at the Hague. Wilhelmus had seven children, four of whom were living as late as 1301.

There are then no records of the family until 1346 when Heinrich Schenck van Nydeck (1A)* is mentioned. He was a grandson of Wilhelmus, but there is no information as to which of the latter's sons was Heinrich's father. In the year 1359, the lords, knights and yeomen of the counties of Geldern and Cleve concluded a treaty, in which Heinrich was assessed "four men and horses, completely equipped and armed." On January 13, 1379, he offered to the Duke of Cleve, the privileges of his castle of Afferden. He sold, July 12, 1389, to Elbricht van Eyll, son of Evert, the court of Munster, afterwards called Munster Mannshof, situated in the county of Geldern.

Heinrich Schenck van Nydeck was Lord of Afferden, a small village in the province of Geldern, and was also Feoffer of Wachtendonk. He married Aleid van Rayde who inherited the castle of Walbeck, thus bringing that estate into the Schenck family. One-half of all the revenues of Walbeck were transferred, in 1381, to the Duke of Geldern, Wilhelm van Julich, in return for which the Duke was to protect and defend the village and parish as if his own. Heinrich had two sons, Wynand and Heinrich (3A), and one daughter, Lisbeth. The latter became a nun at Gravendael. She provided annually for the Convent of Gaesdonk, "thirty-

---

*NOTE.—The numbers following the names correspond to those used in Part II, and serve to identify the individuals.

three pairs of shoes, upon the condition that they be given every year on St. Martin's, by the prior and the convent, to the poor, namely: eleven pairs to poor males, eleven pairs to poor females, and eleven pairs to poor boys and girls to age of fifteen years." For this she gave to the convent for a number of years, seventy golden guilders.

There is no record as to the date of Heinrich's death, but we know that the family estates were divided December 31, 1403. The elder son, Wynand, received Afferden, while the younger son, Heinrich, was given some revenues, the court Ten Broke in Kampen and an estate at Ottersum. Walbeck and other property not mentioned in the division, the parents designated should go, after their death, to the sons. Wynand, however, renounced his equity and gave to Heinrich his share "of the house Walbeck with its outhouses, orchards and gardens, just as it stands and is situated within its ditches and limits." Wynand purchased Blyenbeck in 1405. He married Aleid van Bellinghoven and they had one son, who died young. The titles and estates, therefore, went to the younger brother Heinrich (3A) who thus became Lord of Afferden, Walbeck and Blyenbeck, Feoffer of Wachtendonk and Bailiff of Geldern. There is a record of his marriage and of his death, which occurred December 8, 1452. He and his wife, were, as especial benefactors of the convent of Gaesdonk, declared entitled to all the good offices on the part of the convent and promise was given them that holy mass was to be read daily for all time and eternity, for the benefit of their souls.

On the death of Heinrich, in 1452, the estates went
to the eldest of Heinrich's three children, Diederich (5A),
who became possessed of very considerable property in
addition to his inheritance. As heir of the Knight Goesen
Stek, he received the house Cradenborch and appurte-
nances and all of his estate with their complete rights and
privileges. Like his father and aunt Lisbeth, he became
a benefactor of the convent of Gaesdonk, giving on June
1, 1443, an estate, Hazengest, in Baerls, the revenues of
which were to be used for the benefit of the convent.
Of his eleven children, two became monks and three
nuns. He died in 1487 and August 7th of that year
the estate was divided, Derick (11A), the fourth son,
receiving some of the less important property. However,
on the death of his brothers, he inherited their share and
became Lord of Afferden and Blyenbeck. He had two
morganatic wives, Catherine Rutgen and Gertgen Brugers, and later married Alheit Custers, of Arssen.

For the next seventy years there waged a contest for
the estate of Derick. Derick's eldest brother, Winand
(8A), had a daughter, Adelheid by name, who married
for her second husband, Diderick van der Lippe, Lord
of Betgenhausen. He was a trusty retainer of the Duke
Carl van Egmont, and no sooner had he secured the
hand of the widow than he began his designs against the
estate of the family. In this he was aided by one Godart
Haes, who was a follower of the Archbishop of Cologne,
and who had married Catherine, Lady van Huls, a daughter of Petronella Schenck van Nydeck (13A), a sister
of Derick. These two men, supported by their influential
and powerful superiors, caused an immense amount of

trouble for the Schenck family. They based their claim
on the allegation that Derick's marriage to Alheit Custers
was illegal on account of a relationship in the third
degree between Alheit and Gertgen Brugers.

The dispute was carried to the Pope at Rome and was
before the courts of the Netherlands for many years.
Rome rendered its final decision in 1546, against the
children of Derick, while the civil courts had issued
decrees in their favor. The matter was carried to the
Emperor Charles V., who declared the lawsuit at Cologne
and its sentence void, and ordered the children of Derick
to comply with the sentence passed at Rome and desist
disputing possession of the estates. This decision was
"given in our imperial capital, Spain, the 21st of October
in the year of our Lord, 1549."

However, from 1559 until the death of Martin
Schenck van Nydeck (29A), in 1589, during which
years the war between Spain and the Netherlands tore
the country into shreds, there was constant fighting
between the forces of Martin and those of van der Lippe
for possession of Blyenbeck. These knights were first
on the one side and then on the other, Martin for the
most part fighting against Spain and catholicism, for the
sake of the Netherlands and protestantism.

Many interesting events in the life of Martin are
related by Motley in his *The United Netherlands* and
in the pamphlet *The Blyenbeck and Afferden Branch of
the Family of Schenck van Nydeck,* an excerpt from the
Family of Schenck van Nydeggen, published in Cologne
in 1860. At the time of Martin's death, Blyenbeck was

in the hands of the Spanish, and after much trouble Caspar van der Lippe, a son of Diderick van der Lippe, received an order from the Prince of Parma that the Spanish garrison should leave Blyenbeck and restore it to Caspar. A daughter of Caspar became heiress to the estate and by her marriage with Christoffle Schenck van Nydeck, Lord van Hillenrath, carried the ancient estates to that branch of the family.

During these troublesome times Peter Schenck van Nydeck (30A), was a follower of his more famous brother, Martin. Peter's son, Martin (35A), is said to have emigrated with his children to America, but no trace of him has been found in this country. It is likely that the misfortunes and reverses which overtook the family caused them to seek anew their fortunes in the land of promise—the Nieu Netherlands.

EARLY AMERICAN HISTORY.

The immigrant ancestor of Rulef Schenck was Roelof Martense Schenck, who was born at Amersfoort, Holland, in 1619. Misfortunes had overtaken the family during the almost constant wars which occurred during the sixteenth century in the Netherlands and in addition the Emperor Charles V. had, after seventy years, rendered a decision which was adverse to Roelof's grandfather, Peter (30A)*, thus depriving this branch of the family of the title to the ancestral estates. Roelof's grand-

---

*NOTE—The numbers following the names are the same as appear in Part II. and serve to identify the individuals.

uncle, Sir Martin Schenck van Nydeck, was heir to the castle of Blyenbeck, but the title was contested by his cousin, Caspar van der Lippe, and Martin was besieged in his castle. After a long campaign, Martin was ousted. His brother Peter, a gallant soldier, who had supported Sir Martin, lost favor with the authorities and was deprived of the greater part of his possessions. Thus it was that Peter's son, with his children, sought to renew his fortune by coming to the Nieu Netherlands.

It is probable that Roelof with his brother, Jan, and sister, Anetje, sailed in the ship "de Valckner," arriving in New Amsterdam, June 28, 1650. That they arrived some time during 1650 is certain, as will be shown later. In this ship came also Jacob van Couwenhoven, who with Adrian van der Donck and Jan Eversten Bout, had made a contract with the West India Company, dated at Amsterdam, March 19, 1650, to take "to the Nieu Netherlands, before 1st June, prox., 200 passengers, 100 to be farmers, and farm servants, and 100 such as the Amsterdam Chamber usually send over."

Roelof lived for a few years in Breuklyn and in 1660 married Neeltje Geretsen van Couwenhoven, a niece of Jacob van Couwenhoven. He then settled at Amersfoort (later Flatlands), Long Island, where he resided until his death in 1704, and where he is buried.

In the early colonial records of the New Netherlands, Roelof's name first appears in connection with a grant of land at Amersfoort, consisting of twenty-three morgans, or about forty-six acres. This grant is dated January 29, 1661. In 1664, he was one of the magistrates of the five towns on Nassau Island (Long Island) who joined in a protest against the outrages of the English. The Director-General called a meeting of delegates at Midwout, February 26, 1664, and they then made accusations against the English Captain Scott and voted a remonstrance. It was in this year that the English took over the government of New Amsterdam and the so-called Knickerbocker rule ceased.

The English required new patents to be taken out and the following patent for the town of Amersfoort was issued by Governor Richard Nicoll:—

RICHARD NICHOLL, Esq., Gov., &c., &c.: *Whereas,* there is a certain town within this Government situate and being in the West Riding of Yorkshire upon Long Island, commonly called or known by ye name of Amersfoort, als. Flattlands, which said town is now in ye tenure or occupation of several freeholders and inhabitants who have heretofore been seated there by authority, and likewise made lawful purchasers of ye granted part of ye lands thereunto belonging, have also improved the greater part thereof, and settled a competent number of families thereupon; *Now* for a confirmation unto ye Freeholders and inhabitants of the premises, *Know ye,* that by virtue of ye *Commission* and *Authority* unto me given by His Royal Highness, I have given, ratified, confirm and grant unto Elbert Elbertse (Stoothoff), Gerrit Loockemans, Roelof Martense (Schenck), Pieter Claes (Wyckoff), Wellem Gerrits (van Couwenhoven), Tho. Hillebrants, Stephen Coerten (van Voorhees), and Coert Stephens (van Voorhees), as *Patentees* for and on behalf of themselves and their associates, ye Freeholders and inhabitants of ye said town, their heirs, successors and assigns, All ye tract together with ye several parcels, &c.

MATHIAS, Secretary.

(Signed)   RICHARD NICHOLL. (L. S.)

Fort James, 4th October, 1667, etc.

Governor Cleve appointed Roelof Schenck one of the Schepens for Flatlands, August 18, 1673, and October 25th of the same year, he was chosen a lieutenant of militia. He was a deputy to the council held at the city hall in New Amsterdam, March 26, 1674.

In volume II. of the *Documentary History of New York,* a valuation of property shows that Roelof Schenck possessed 2 polls, 4 horses, 1 do. of —— years old, 10 cows, 2 do. of 2 years old, 4 do. of 1 year old, 3 hogs :— Total 152 pounds, 14 shillings. Also 52 morgans of valley land, 104 pounds. Total 256 pounds, 14 shillings.

He was next to the wealthiest man in town and sixth or seventh on Long Island in point of possessions. In 1698 he had four slaves.

The inhabitants of the New Netherlands were required to take the oath of allegiance to the English king and these documents show whether the individual was a native or an immigrant. If the latter, the length of residence in the New Netherlands was given. Roelof took this oath of allegiance in 1687 and it is stated that he and his brother, Jan, had been "thirty-seven years in the country," thus confirming the date of arrival as 1650.

There are documents showing that Roelof was commissioned a justice of Kings County in 1689 and a Captain of Horse in 1690.

Roelof was three times married. His first wife, by whom he had six children, Martin, Annetje, Jonica, Marike, Jan and Gerret Roelofse, died in 1673. Two years later, he married Anetje Pieterse Wyckoff, by whom he had four children, Margaretta, Neeltje, Mayke and

Sara. The date of the death of the second wife is unknown. In 1688, however, Roelof married Catrina Crigers, widow of Christopher Hoogland. This marriage contract is of interest. A translation of the original Dutch document is as follows:—

Today, date underwritten, Mr. Roelof Martensen Schenck, widower of the late Anneke Pieters, on the one side, and Mrs. Catherine Creugiers, widow of the late Christopher Hoogland on the other side, declared that they had agreed between themselves to the honor of God, to enter into matrimony; but before the solemnization thereof, they had convened that the same should be confirmed in following manner, to wit: That the aforesaid bridegroom shall bring for the maintenance of himself and his future wife such property as by the blessing of God he has become possessed of; nothing excepted; but he shall not acquire any ownership in the estate and property of the aforesaid future bride nor in those which she shall obtain hereafter; and that the future bride shall bring nothing into the wedded state for the maintenance of the couple, but out of the estate and property of her future husband she and her son Hermanus Hoogland, shall be supported and maintained in board and clothing as is decent and proper. It is further conditioned and stipulated that her property, moveable and immoveable, present and future, nothing excepted, shall not be held in commonalty with the estate and property of the aforesaid bridegroom, but that she shall keep and administer her estate separately, either personally or by others, and dispose of it as she shall think fit without the future bridegroom having or claiming any guardianship, order, or administration over her estate against her will or pleasure, but that all this property with its increments and gains shall remain her own forever and subject to testamentary disposition; and after her decease to her children and their lawful descendants.

Subject to the above written conditions, an inventory shall be taken of the property of the future bride and signed by both and attached hereto; which inventory the future man and wife desire to be so binding and inviolable as if the same was herein mentioned and inserted. It is further stipulated and conditioned that if the bridegroom should first die the aforesaid future bride shall throughout her life, whether she remains single or marries again, remain in full possession and usufruct of his bowery bought from the widow and heirs of Govert Lockermans with the house, orchard, negroes, one half of the horses and cattle found there; provided that out of the revenue thereof she shall keep it in good condition without being held responsible and accountable in any manner for misfortunes; provided further: that she shall maintain and support, educate and have instructed in reading and writing, and taught a trade to which they are adapted, the minor children now then living who shall then live, and the child or children which they together may beget, and after the death of the said bride all the property, viz: Bowery, said house, farm, orchard, negroes, horses and cattle shall be subject to the disposition and order of the aforesaid bridegroom; but in case the future bride should die before her aforesaid bridegroom she shall have no right to claim anything beyond her clothing of silk, woolen and linen and her jewels which she has used and owned during her lifetime, out of the estate and property of the aforesaid bridegroom, than a decent burial. It is further expressly conditioned and stipulated, that on account of any debts and obligations contracted before the date of proposed marriage by either of the parties hereto, the other one shall not be dunned, molested or called upon, much less shall they be legally collected, as all community of property and debts between the parties aforesaid is hereby expressly excluded and disclaimed.

This Contract of Marriage has been agreed upon and concluded under the above conditions; and the bridegroom binds himself, his executors, administrators, heirs and descendants that it shall have full effect under the aforesaid stipulations and conditions, and to make it still more binding, the aforesaid bride has chosen for her assistant and Trustee in this matter her son Derick Hoogland with his heirs and descendants to receive the above for the behoof of the said bride and her heirs and for.

the behoof of nobody else; and, furthermore, the said bridegroom binds himself and promises for himself and for his executors, administrators and heirs and descendants to give, satisfy and allow to enjoy, the said Derick Hoogland as chosen Trustee of the aforesaid bride, or his heirs and descendants, all which has hereinbefore been convened and agreed for and to the behoof of the aforesaid bride or her heirs and for the behoof of nobody else, anything heretofore done or agreed upon to the contrary notwithstanding, either in law or outside of law thereto appertaining. This done, agreed and concluded at New York and for its further confirmation, it is signed and sealed by them the 9th of November, 1688.

CATRYNTYNA CRIGERS. (Seal)
ROELOF MARTENSEN. (Seal)

Attested: WILLEM BOGARDUS,
Notary Public.

Witnesses:
NICHOLAS GERRET.
CORNELIUS DIRCKSEN.

Roelof Martense Schenck died, either in 1704 or 1705. The records of the late Garret C. Schenck give the date as 1705, while Lieut. A. D. Schenck, in his *Rev. William Schenck, His Ancestry and Descendants,* from which most of the foregoing facts are taken, states that the date was 1704. At all events, his will was probated August 3, 1705, and may be found in the New York Surrogate's Office, liber 7, pp. 209. It is as follows:—

In the name of God Amen,—ye fourth day of September in ye third year of ye reign of our Sovereign Lady Annie now of England &c., Queen, and in ye year of our Lord one thousand seven hundred and four,—I, Roelof Schenck, of Flatlands, in Kings County, on Nassau Island, in the Colony of New York—being of good and perfect memory—praised be Almighty God, therefore doe make this, my last Will and Testament in manner and form following—that is to say:

First, recommending my soul unto Almighty God who gave it, and my body to ye earth to be buried in such decent and Christianlike manner and in such place as by my Executor, hereafter named, shall be thought fitt and convenient—hoping for a glorious resurrection at the last day.

Item—I give, grant, devise, and bequeath unto my loving wife Catharine Schenck, for and during her natural life, all my farm or tenement at Flatlands aforesaid, now in my possession and whereon I now live with ye House, Garden, Barne, orchard, and premises thereunto belonging. To have, hold, occupy, and enjoy for her use only, without impeachment of waste—for and during her natural life—and all according to a contract and agreement made between my said wife Catharine and myself before marriage, bearing date ye ninth day of November, 1688, reference being thereunto had, may at large appear. Provided, always, that if my said wife Catharine happens to re-marry after my decease, then my gift, grant, devise and bequeath aforesaid, to be null and voyd to all intents and purposes.

Item—I give, grant, devise, and bequeath unto my loving son Martin Schenck, his heyres and assigns, forever, after the decease or re-marriage of my said wife Catharine, all my Houses, Lands, Tenements, orchards, Gardens, meadows, and hereditaments in Possession, Reversion, or Remainder, Either within the Town and Libertyes of Flatlands aforesaid, or elsewhere. To Have and To Hold all ye said Houses and lands as afore exprest unto the said Martin Schenck, his heirs and assigns forever, upon this condition, he paying the legacies hereafter mentioned unto my children hereafter named, within six years after possession taken by him—the said Martin—of my houses and lands aforesaid. That is to say—to my daughter Jonica, sixty-four pounds and ten shillings in money—to my daughter Mayke—sixty-four pounds and ten shillings in money—to my son John, sixty-four pounds and ten shillings in money—to my son Garrett sixty-four pounds and ten shillings in money—to my daughter Margrieta sixty-four pounds and ten shillings in money—to my daughter Neltie sixty-four pounds and ten shillings in money—to my daughter Mayke sixty-four pounds and ten shillings in money—

to my daughter Sara sixty-four pounds and ten shillings in money—and to ye two children of my daughter Anneke deceased, by name Roeloft and Albert, each ten pounds in money—and farther it is my will that said legacys be paid to ye legatees aforesaid within six years time as aforementioned and that those of the legatees that are in most need or want shall be first payed, always provided that if my son Martin refuses, denyes or delays to pay ye legacys above mentioned—then my houses and lands above exprest to be equally divided among my children aforementioned and sold to the highest bidder.

Item—I give, grant, devise, and bequeath unto my loving children by name Martin, Jonica, Marike, John, Garrett, Margrieta, Neltie, Mayke, and Sarah, their executors and assigns forever after ye decease or remaryage of my said wife Catharine, all and singular my goods and Chattels, rights and credits, whatsoever or whensoever the same are, or shall become due in equal proportion be divided between them, that is to say, the one-half immediately after my decease and the other half after my wife's decease or remaryage as aforesaid, and that there be an Inventory taken of all my goods and Chattels soon after my decease by my Executors hereafter named. That my children or creditors may not be defrauded, and that my said wife Catharine shall give in bond and security to deliver or cause to be delivered upon her remaryage or death to my children above named what goods and chattels she shall enjoy as ye one-half part thereof, death of living creatures and wearing out of goods only excepted; and farther, it is my will that my daughter Sarah aforesaid, before any division of ye moveables have a good outsetting equal as my other children have had, and then to share equally with the rest, and that my son Martin, for his birthright as Eldest son, shall have my negro boy Anthony, my said wife only to have ye profit or use of ye one-half of ye labor or service of said boy during her life time or remaryage.

I do hereby make, appoint, and ordain my loving son, Martin Schenck, whole and sole Executor of this my last Will and Testament to see it performed according to ye true intent and meaning thereof. In witness whereof, I, the said Roelof Schenck, have hereunto set my hand and seal ye day and year first above written.

(Signed)   ROELOF SCHENCK, [L. S.]

Signed, sealed and delivered in the presence of us:

COERT STEVENSE.
GARRET STOOTHOFF.
HENRY FILKIN.

The next in our line of descent is the fifth child and second son of Roelof (1a), namely Jan Schenck (6a). Born at Flatlands, L. I., in 1670, he married Sara Willemse van Couwenhoven in 1692. Subsequently, Jan's sisters, Margaretta and Neeltje, married brothers of Sara. In 1698, Jan removed to a tract of land in Pleasant Valley, near Holmdel, New Jersey. This tract, consisting of 500 acres, had been purchased from John Brown, a merchant of Middletown, N. Y., in 1696, by Cornelius van Couwenhoven (who later married Jan's sister, Margaretta), Coert van Voorhees and Peter Wyckoff. The two latter sold out their equity to Garret and Jan and the tract was divided into three farms,* those of Garret (7a) and Jan Schenck and their future brother-in-law, Cornelius van Couwenhoven. At the corner where these three farms met was dedicated a plot, containing about one-half acre of land, for a family bury-

---

*NOTE.—These farms were visited by Adrian A. Schenck in 1883. I find among his notes the following:—"In August, 1883, I visited the house in which Jan and Sara lived. Only a part, the sitting room and adjoining bedroom, remains. The door jams were hewn from pine logs, and dressed down with a plane, no saw having been used. The bedroom door was in one piece, hewn from a log, and on the inside was painted the coat of arms of the van Couwenhoven family, still quite distinct. In the burying ground were some 20 graves, marked either Schenck or Couwenhoven."—B. R. S.

ing ground. It was afterwards also used by other families.

From Garret Schenck has descended a very large branch of the family, including a number of illustrious men, among them the Rev. William Schenck; General William C. Schenck, who was prominent in the war of 1812, and who first surveyed and founded Port Lawrence, now Toledo, Ohio; Col. William Rogers Schenck; Admiral James Findlay Schenck; General Robert C. Schenck, Minister to Brazil, Congressman from Ohio, Minister to England; Lieutenant Woodhull S. Schenck, U. S. N.; and Lieutenant Alexander D. Schenck, U. S. A.

But little can be learned concerning the life of Jan and Sara. For over fifty years they lived on their New Jersey farm, bringing up a family of four sons and six daughters.

The first of these sons was Roelof (12a), born at Flatlands, L. I., in 1692, and at the age of six years going, with the family, from Long Island to New Jersey. He lived on the farm of his father and was apparently a well known man in the community. The only information we have concerning him is to be found in a small volume, published in 1905, edited by The Rev. A. I. Martine of Marlborough, N. J., and entitled *Bi-Centennial Celebration of the Reformed Church of the Navasink and Its Two Branches (1699-1899)*. A majority of the settlers of the present Monmouth County, New Jersey, came from Long Island, and these families, with a few others, constituted the congregation to which the Long Island pastors ministered. Stated preaching was begun in 1699, various ministers coming from Long Island, but finding their duties exceedingly burdensome "because of the distance they were compelled to travel, and the danger of crossing the great bay in small boats." This continued for ten years when the Reformed Church of Freehold and Middletown (the Congregation of the Navasink) was organized. The Consistory was composed of Peter van Deventer and John Wyckoff, elders, and Jacob van Dorn and Garret Schenck, deacons. In 1714, the parsonage, consisting of a house and a tract of "one hundred acres of good arable land, as good as any in Freehold, on which a family may subsist comfortably," was conveyed by Jacobus Romain, to John Schenck and Cornelius Couwenhoven of Middletown, and Peter Tyson of Freehold, in trust for the use of the congregation. It was located "five quarters of an hour's distance from the church." The first edifice—probably used both as a school and a church—termed by the Dutch, "Gabat House," or prayer house, was located near by, on Hendrickson's Hill. The first pastor was Rev. Guillaume Bertholf, the second, Rev. Joseph Morgan, who served until 1731, when the Rev. Gerardus Haeghoort was called from Holland. The next year it was decided to erect a new edifice. The congregation, however, was so evenly divided on the question of where the new church should be located that they agreed that it should be built on the site to which the first load of stone for building purposes was carted. It was late in the afternoon when the meeting adjourned, but "Mr. Roelof Schenck (12a), more frequently called "Black Roelof," immediately went home, hitched up his team, gathered the stones and carted them to the lot on which the building now stands." That settled the matter.

The edifice which was then built was in use over ninety years and was taken down in 1826 to make room for the present church, the Old Brick Church of Marlborough.

For many years there were no pews in the original church. The congregation sat on benches, the men around the wall, the women in the center. Some used double chairs, such as were generally used in wagons in those days. Some of the families would ride to church sitting on these chairs, and then, taking them out of their wagons, would carry them into the church for use during service. A great many would go on horseback; one horse generally carried a man and his wife, and very frequently a baby also. Carriages were unknown and farm wagons without springs were thought to be comfortable. There was no means of heating the church, for stoves were not in existence. Private houses were made warm by the use of large fireplaces, but churches were built without chimneys. The women brought with them small foot-stoves, which kept their feet warm, while good homespun cloth in ample folds protected their persons.

Roelof Schenck (12a) was frequently called "Black Roelof" to distinguish him from a cousin of the same name. He was of a swarthy complexion, was large, muscular and very strong. The following anecdote is told of him. According to the tradition, a professional prize fighter having heard of Roelof's strength, sought to obtain a match and prove his superiority. He paid him a visit and encountered Roelof as the latter was returning from the fields with the plow on his shoulder. Engaging in conversation, Roelof placed the plow on the ground; becoming deeply interested as the talk continued, he grasped the handle of the plow in one hand, and holding it at arm's length like a cane, used it to point out the various places of interest. The prize fighter looked on in utter amazement, then suddenly remembered that he wished to see another man by the name of Schenck, and started out to find him.

Roelof (12a) died January 19, 1766, and was buried in the old burying ground at Pleasant Valley. In August, 1883, the stone was still standing and a sassafras tree, more than five inches in diameter, was growing from the center of the grave. On the stone appeared the following:—

"Here Lies Interred the Body of Roelof Schenck, Son of John, who Departed this Life the Nineteenth of January in the Year of Our Lord, One Thousand Seven Hundred and Sixty-six, aged Seventy-three Years, Ten Months and Twenty-eight Days."

By the side of this stone was another giving the record of the death of his wife, Geesie.

We have little information concerning John Schenck (24a), the third child and first son of Roelof (12a), beyond the facts of his birth, marriage and death. Born January 22, 1720, he married when twenty-one years of age, Jacamyntie van Couwenhoven, who was some two years his senior. They had two sons and one daughter.

The first son, Rulief, married Sarah Lippert, had three sons, and about 1800 removed to Ohio, locating near Cincinnati. John Schenck (24a) died June 27, 1749. His gravestone bears the following inscription:—

"Here Lies the Body of John Schenck, who Departed this Life, June 27, Anno Domini, 1749, Aged Twenty-nine Years, Two Months and Five Days."

This would make his birthday April 22, 1720, and not January 22, as given in the records.

Cornelius Schenck (28a), the second son of John (24a), was born September 19, 1744, and for some years lived on a farm in Pleasant Valley, Monmouth County, New Jersey. For some reason he left this farm and removed to a farm near Charleston, Montgomery County, New York, a few miles south of the present city of Fonda. The date of the removal is uncertain, but it was apparently subsequent to 1776, as all of his children were born in New Jersey, Rulef, the youngest, being born in that year. The probable cause of the removal was the barrenness of the New Jersey land, which before the discovery of marl, was most unproductive. Two amusing anecdotes are told in connection with Cornelius and his Jersey farm. Soon after he had located there, two of his relatives rode over on horseback to see him. In those days all the farm buildings were erected in the center of the farm, without regard to the highway, and the buildings were surrounded by a door yard. After riding across the fields and coming into the yard, the two visitors dismounted and one of them throwing his bridle over his arm, began walking about as though look-

ing for something, at the same time apparently crying.
When asked what the trouble was, he replied—"It is
really too bad, too bad; Cornelius is here on a farm so
poor that it won't raise a mullin stalk to tie one's horse
to."

About the time Cornelius was leaving for New York
State, the same relative, lamenting the sad condition of
affairs, remarked, "too bad, too bad, Cornelius continues
in such bad luck; he has left a farm too poor to produce
a mullin stalk and gone into New York State where the
stones are so thick there isn't room for a mullin stalk
to grow."   Whether the latter statement was descrip-
tive of the new location, or only a fancy of the wag, is
not known.

Cornelius Schenck (28a) and his wife, Margaret Taylor, had six children. The first son, John, removed to
Cayuga County, brought up a family of fourteen children
and died at Springport, June 8, 1850. The youngest
son was Rulef, all of whose descendants we propose to
trace in a subsequent chapter. Cornelius died January
14, 1790.

It will be noted that Rulef represents the sixth generation in America and the fourteenth of the generations
whose unbroken records we possess. In some of the
descendant families of Rulef there are now children of
the eleventh generation in America and the nineteenth
from Heinrich Schenck van Nydeck.

Little is known of the boyhood of Rulef, and we have
no record as to when he came to Charleston. In 1802

ELSIE BAIRD SCHENCK
1785-1857

RULEF SCHENCK
1776-1852

he married Elsie Baird,* and the first six of their eleven children were born in Montgomery County. In 1814, when 38 years of age, he made a journey westward and purchased a tract of land in Lysander Township, Onondaga County. In April, 1815, he removed to this property, then in the midst of the wilderness. When cleared, it proved to be productive and Rulef became a successful and prosperous farmer. He reared a family of eleven children and helped all of them, more or less, to a start in life. He resided on this farm until his death, which occurred April 15, 1852.

Rulef Schenck and his wife Elsie (Baird) Schenck are buried at the cemetery in Plainville.

A brief sketch of the early history of Onondaga County and a few of its villages in Lysander Township may not be out of place at this point.

Originally, all that part of New York State situated west of Schoharie County comprised Montgomery County. In 1789, the territory west of a north and south line running through Seneca Lake was set off and called Ontario

---

*NOTE.—We have but meager information concerning Elsie Baird and her family. The family first appeared in Monmouth County, New Jersey, about 1680. The first of the name was named John. Tradition relates that he introduced a new method of courtship. John chanced one day to meet in the woods Mary Hall, whom he afterwards married. As both were bashful, they halted at some distance from one another under a tree. It was love at first sight, and in a short time John, who was a Quaker, broke the painful silence, by saying, "If thou wilt marry me, say yea; if thou wilt not, say nay." Mary said "yea" and proved a noble wife and mother.

It is presumed that Elsie Baird's family removed from New Jersey to Montgomery County, New York, between 1780 and 1800, but I have no information concerning the date. The Baird family in the vicinity of Fonda and Gloversville is a large one, and reunions are held annually, usually at Sacandaga Park.

County. In 1791, Herkimer County was formed from the western part of Montgomery and comprised the portion of Herkimer lying west of Whitestown, and east of Seneca Lake. In 1794, the original Onondaga County was formed by the present counties of Cortland, Cayuga, Onondaga and Seneca with parts of Wayne, Oswego, Thompkins and Schuyler, and it was not until 1816 that Onondaga County assumed its present size.

Baldwinsville was founded in the spring of 1807, when Dr. James C. Baldwin built a dam and erected a mill there. The settlement was first called *Columbia,* but in 1817, in which year the post office was established, the name of *Baldwin's Bridge* was given to the village. The present name was, however, preferred by the residents, and it later became recognized by the post office department. The town was very prosperous until 1819, when the opening of the Erie Canal diverted much of the commerce which previously had passed through the Seneca River, and for a time the village's growth was retarded.

The village was incorporated June 3, 1848.

The first newspaper in this part of the country was started by Samuel B. West in 1844, under the name of the *Baldwinsville Republican.* Two years later it became the property of C. M. Hosmer, who changed the name to the *Onondaga Gazette.* In 1878 it became, and has since remained, the *Baldwinsville Gazette.* Its files contain a wealth of local matter of interest to the historian.

Plainville, located in the western part of the Township of Lysander, was originally called *Wilson's Corners,* from the fact that William Wilson located there in 1806.

Other early settlers were A. B. Scofield, Elias Scofield, David Carroll, and Peter Voorhees, grandfather of James L. Voorhees of Baldwinsville. Abram Daily, Marvin Adams, Rulef Schenck and John Bratt located nearby in 1815 and 1816. When the post office was opened in 1821, the inhabitants suggested the name *Farmersville*, but there was another office in the state by this name and the department designated the place Plainville. Mr. Stoddard, Simon Town, John Buck, B. B. Schenck and Lyman Norton were the early postmasters. The mail was received and dispatched weekly and came through the Camillus office.

The first school house was erected in 1819 and Amos Adams was the first teacher. The Christian Church was organized in 1820; the edifice, built in 1831, was burned in April, 1852, and replaced by the present structure in 1854. For thirty-nine years, until 1876, the people looked to Dr. B. B. Schenck for medical service.

Lysander was settled in 1811, being first called *Vickery's Corners,* from several families of that name who located there. In 1817, Chauncey Betts established there a general store, built a small distillery and erected a potash factory. It then became known as *Bett's Corners,* until the establishment of a post office a few years later. Among the early settlers of this section were W. P. Bump, Richard Smith, Grover Buel, Abram van Doren and Alfred Smith.

No better description of the pioneer days of Lysander and of the people who lived there can be given than that which was read by Dr. B. B. Schenck at a family gathering in 1881. On October 13th. of that year a reunion was held at the residence of John Schenck, in Plainville, attended by four brothers and four sisters of the eleven children of Rulef Schenck. After dinner, Benjamin Baird Schenck read the following:—

The present gathering is at the end of a long series of years and with some of us it furnishes an opportunity for a retrospect of nearly two-thirds of a century.

The review with me, as respects our immediate family, opens with the vision of a train of five wagons, loaded with household effects, moving westward. One wagon carried the head of the family with the children, six in number, and his niece, our cousin. We were journeying from a region occupied for several years to the far off West, and though then very young in years, I have a memory of the moving procession made very solemn by the spoken farewells of parting friends, and particularly of a father and mother with children and grand children.

The tardy movements of the vehicles along the muddy roads of a March season, (the frost but lately going out of the ground making places almost mirey) made probable a slow and tedious journey.

The season of the year, March 8, 1815, was the time for expected rough and disagreeable weather. The distance to be traveled, 120 miles, which was duly made in nine days, is now made in nine hours.

Starting from a locality in Montgomery County, some six or seven miles south of the Mohawk River, town of Charleston, we came that day to its very banks. Then we drove westward to the fabled region of fever, ague and Indians, in the far off Onondaga County. This was before the days of steam and electricity, those annihilators of space and time.

The new locality, but a mile or so from this very spot, furnished a hospitable domicil, a log house, for us to occupy. That spot had been secured by purchase in advance of our coming, so that the tenure of the place was not doubtful; indeed, it furnished permanently the place of residence for both our parents for the balance of their worthy lives—the one for 37 years, and the other for 42 years—and is still the residence of Rulef, the youngest born, but how changed!

Then the unappropriated wilds furnished pasturage of leeks and leaves for the stock and the ample range in territory, with the adventurous inclination to wander therein, made necessary the clanging cow-bell; hours of search and hunt were often necessary, and miles of travel gone over to return them to the fold.

Myself, at first too young for this particular pursuit, it was duly performed by the older ones, often by him who now furnishes the invitation to this family gathering. The extent of wilderness being nearly the whole domain, rendered this peregrination extremely lonesome and tiresome. The heavy growth of stinging nettles, now nearly obsolete, were frightful impediments to the often, if not always, barefooted boy. The hooting owl and buzzing partridge suddenly breaking the gloomy silence of the dense forest, would thrill the hunter with emotions such as fright gives to broken contemplations.

The people, or neighbors as we say, were those living any distance off, either in the town or out of it. Neighborhood was not the exact word, an individual dweller not making a neighborhood. Joseph Howe, of whom our father purchased, had just left the premises, but I could name a David Carrol, a land holder, who would have been a farmer if he had given his time to working the soil instead of fishing and hunting; also a Simon Town and a William Wilson, whose son William, one year after, viz., April 14, 1816, took to him for wife, our esteemed cousin, Polly Shepard. She fell a victim to the incidents and frailties of life and left him and us in 1826; and of the same neighbor Wilson, his son Alfred took, December 22, 1820, one of our sisters, Sally, from our household, for his life companion. That association and companionship continued for some 35 years, when he was called by death to leave behind her, who so long had kindly ministered to his every want. Aged now, and widowed over 27 years, she is with us today, the eldest of the group.

I could name an Abram Dailey, who was soon followed by a John Bratt, whose son Peter, in due course of time, March 1827, came into the family for a place and relation, and worthily he sustained that relation for 46 years, when death severed him from us. A year or so later, our sister Margaret, his consort, yielded to disease and followed him, January 31, 1875.

I also readily recognize a Peter Voorhees, whose family in later times was prominent in all these parts, and whose grandson, James L., by marriage with Eleanor, our niece, the daughter of our present host, gave him a relationship to our family. Eleanor in a few short years of aggravated suffering, sank into her quiet grave. James L. changed his widowed state in a couple of years, by marriage to Sarah C., our niece, youngest daughter of sister Margaret and Peter Bratt.

West of us, across the Great Bear Swamp, came the muffled sounds of ox drivers, log rollers and ax men—of a Sanborn, a Critchet, a Van Blaricom, a Hulet, a Bartlett, a Wright, and later a Marselus, a Carncross, a Van Horn, a Simmons, a Relyea, a Morrill and others, a succession to the present time. The whoop of the lost cow hunter in the late evenings, was replied to by other whoops, or by pounding with a beetle or an ax on a hollow log lying at the wood pile. Again I turn my eye southward and I spy an Elijah Snow, with his little whisky distillery on the bank near where now lives B. F. Davis. I see a Stoddard just north, and recognize in him the first Post Master for our present post office, viz. Plainville. As a post office is the most public institution of any in the country, the frequency of the mails is the best announcer of such a recognition. This received a weekly mail bag, carried on horse back, and put up at Camillus, coming through Canal, (now Memphis) and terminating at Lysander and return, all on Saturday of each week.

I see at a glance right here the succession of Post Masters for this office. Next to Stoddard, William Wilson, Simon Town, John Buck, B. B. Schenck, Lyman Norton, and B. B. Schenck, the present incumbent. Before Simon Town was Post Master, we received our mail at Lysander and I presume there was not

JOHN SCHENCK

1804-1884

a subscriber to a regular newspaper in the whole delivery of this office for the first ten years. Post riders or others might obtain patrons for papers and deliver them to such patrons without such papers entering the mails. When a small boy, I was gratified by our parents to receive the *Weedsport Sentinel* in my own name, through Herman Pangburn, for a bushel of corn for the paper six months.

A little to the westward of this Stoddard, I see a Daniel Dutcher, a Major Sayles, a Costen, a Whitman and several others. I could not very well forget a Richard Sullivan, a military musician, an officer of the town, and father of daughters enough for four wives, for three of our fraternity. Two of these, Perlina and Parna, the eldest of his family, in succession became the wives of him who is the centre of this gathering, the one, from October 13, 1831, for nearly twenty years, the other, for the brief period of three years.

By a third marriage, in the autumn of 1858, with Mrs. Julia Parsels Hall, he was comforted for nearly twenty-two years, or until April 19, 1880. Her death left him alone for the third time. [He just now tells me that this is fifty years from his first marriage, October 13, 1831.]

Our neighbor Sullivan could not be forgotten, though death took him from us more than twelve years ago. The strong link that binds my memory to him is she, of his worthy daughters Harriet, who has been my prized and loved companion and wife for more than forty-two years, and who by the blessing of God is with me today, the partner of my declining years.

Nor do I fail to remember him, when I review the past, and see in the pathway of a brother, James L., whose union with the daughter of another neighbor, was dissolved by that ruthless monster, Death. His widowed heart was comforted by the youngest of his daughters, N. Maria, with whom he has journeyed on in wedded life for more than thirty years, and both are with us here today.

Not far out of the direction of the last named neighbor, I see an Abram Emerick, who out of a large family of children, furnished, in his youngest child, Emerancy, a fit and worthy consort for our youngest brother Rulef, latest born of our parents, and who today, although far beyond the meridian of life, and after a union of more than thirty-one years is here to indicate the "rear line" in age, of this, one of the pioneer families of the town.

Again in looking for neighbors, I see a John P. Schuyler, with a model number of children for a new country, viz.—fourteen. A Miles Upson, a Garner Smith, a Job Loomis, a Ben Stevens, a Sam Perry, and a James L. Fenner. The last named neighbor furnished two worthy sons for husbands for two of our sisters. F. W., the elder of the two, took from our already lessened throng of family inmates, our lively sister Eleanor S., the eldest born of our parents in this, our new home. Their marriage relations began in 1834 and continued in pleasant harmony till 1876, a period of forty-two years. How long and yet how short! Her widowed heart felt keenly the loss of her genial partner and valued husband. Wearied of the lonesomeness of her so greatly changed situation, and being found by a worthy citizen, Perry H. Hinsdell, of another town (Salina), in this county, whose home had been invaded by the death of a beloved wife, they changed both of their situations, by vowing to each other and receiving the rites matrimonial. They are here present today to affiliate in this commemoration of family friendship and allegiance.

Russel B., the other son, and the younger of the two—as neighbors' sons sometimes will, if well behaved—found a welcome reception to the abode of our parents, where was yet remaining in single life, our blithe and youngest sister, Hannah. With lover's art and brimful worth of character and sense, no wonder of his conquest there. Who would not yield to such attack? He took, as it were, the nest-egg. The household was robbed, so to speak, yet the robber, if he were one, was greeted with the favor of a true friend, yea a family relative. A few brief years, say half-a-dozen, and a feeling of Western advantages operated to change of residence, and October, 1844, found them severing the social surroundings, by removing from the state, the only instance in all this large family of taking up abode outside the state, and but one other outside the county. A fair grade of prosperity attended them. Several times have they in the long thirty-seven years of Michigan life, returned to visit and enliven us. Once he came with the dead body of our Rush (who died at his home in Michigan), that it might be safely guarded on its passage home, so that it might have its long and last rest in the cemetery of his native town.

Now they come to make us a long and may be a final visit, to view again their native soil, to enter the cemeteries of their former home and read from the tomb-stones the well remembered names of former acquaintances, friends and kin—a gloomy pleasantry. But they are here, and right welcome are they too, to all that we can do for their entertainment and enjoyment. Although the final farewells must come, the present is full of genuine pleasure on account of their presence.

I name here, for we cannot forget that other sister, one of the party from the East, the record of whose birth says:—"Catharine Schenck, born February 11, 1806," and though another record says she "died June 21, 1859," yet we all remember her well, and her many years of terrible suffering though not all spent in our presence, affix in our memory indelibly, that one of our number in the lingering thrall of disease, had received the unbroken care of a kind mother while she lived, and when her home was broken up by the death of our parents, another kind sister assumed the task of care and was to her all that a sister could be.

I go again in search of neighbors of that early period, or a little later.

Turning my eyes northwest it meets a Daniel Servoss, a Suel Holton, a Frederick I. Tator, whose youngest daughter Ann L. was for a brief period the wife of our brother, James L. referred to in another part of this review. Then a Josiah Smith, a Dennis Kennedy, a Northrop Preston, a Theophilus Beebe, a Samuel Star, a Richard Smith, a William VanDorn, an Aaron F. Vedder, one of whose sons, James S., became the son-in-law of our host, and with his family now resides in Washington, Kansas. Then a Stuffle Forncrook, a Cornelius Hubbard, a Chauncey Betts, a Cornelius Mount.

These, or most of them have little to do with our history, only to point to them and name them as early residents.

Later on and a little east of some of these, I discern a Garret Vanderveer, and I am reminded that our brother, William B., found and married, January 18, 1843, in the family of this neighbor, a wife, a prize invaluable to him, and accepted, beloved and cherished by us. They journeyed prosperously and happily together for some ten years. His record reads: "W. B. Schenck, born in Lysander November 5, 1819, died in Lysander, March 17, 1853, aged 33 years." Over twenty-seven years have rolled by since the separation, yet the widow has continued and remained in perfect fraternity, presenting and receiving the kindly reciprocities of the entire relationship. Thanks for her willing presence today, for without it, would be a vacuum that she alone can fill, for she only can represent our deceased brother.

Among farmer neighbors and contemporaries, we have found sons-in-laws and daughters-in-law for all but one. About 1830 or '31 came Solomon B. Spaulding, a tradesman of the order of Crispin, and presented inducements acceptable to our sister Eliza, the youngest of Montgomery birth.

He was duly installed, by universal consent, a member of the family, by matrimonial rites, July 14, 1832. His and her struggles in life's controversies were severe, and many of them of doubtful issue. Industry was their habit and hard labor was their fortune, honesty, integrity and hospitality their characteristics. Companionable and well informed, his position in society was well maintained. Many helps and encouragements from him have I received and I know not the time he was not my friend, my fast friend. Nor did I ever enter their door that I did not recognize a hearty welcome from them both, and I know not that any of us can say otherwise. She seemed the nearest to me in age, and though two years my junior her precocity made her almost my equal in the frequent and long searches in the dense and distant forests for the straying cow.

ELIZA SCHENCK SPAULDING

1811-1895

Our memories both run back to that almost dangerous avocation, when we were scarcely more than ten years of age, mere "Babes in the Woods," ever the sister, ever the friend. The words here written may possibly be seen by other eyes, in the coming future, but they will not give the full impression felt then and now by us, so much does each live his own live. How very much would memory suggest, but I forbear. I am always glad to meet you but doubly glad to meet you here today.

Some six years ago a few of us met here to celebrate the seventy-first anniversary of the birth of our host. Then was Solomon with you. You have both been here since, several times perhaps, he in his state of morbid health, and long, almost a wreck. Today he is not here and the reason as stated I copy "Fulton, N. Y., June 13, 1881. Dear Uncle:—Father died at 8 o'clock Saturday night, June 11. His funeral will be at 10 o'clock, Wednesday, at the house. Will be buried at Plainville. Please notify friends."—Mary Phelps.

Widowed at seventy years when almost the period had arrived for your Golden Wedding, only a year or so. Having now reached your three-score years and ten, the allotment to man so often repeated, bare your bereavement, as you have borne all your vicissitudes of life, with fortitude and heroism.

A few statistics and I am done. The years of human life lived by the eleven children of our family sum up 685 years and 8 months. Average age, 62 3-11 years. Of the eleven, eight remain, three are gone! The sum of the ages of the three is 154 years. The average of their age is 51 1-3 years. The sum of the years of the eight remaining is 531 years and 8 months. Average age is 66 years 5 months. The eldest is 78 years 8 months. The youngest is 54 years minus ten days. Yet there has been bereavement and mourning in this family. Hear the necrologic list:

Wives four, sisters two, husbands four, brothers one, equals eleven. Children and nieces ten, children and nephews seven, equals seventeen. Making twenty-eight of those occasions. Add our parents and we have thirty.

We might appropriately say with the pious poet Watts:

> "Save us O! Lord, aloud we pray,
> Nor let our sun go down at noon,
> Thy years are one eternal day,
> And must Thy children die so soon?"

Our sisters given in marriage to our neighbors' sons, and our brothers taking wives from similar sources of neighbors' daughters, somewhat like the Banian tree that has given as many stems and stalks to the family tree. The boughs and branches of these stems or stalks are in a manner covering or shading the territory of and about the original homestead. Their fruits have appeared as the consecutive years have passed. The whole number born to a name is forty-seven, seventeen of whom have gone from off the stage of life, while thirty remain; the latter comparatively sound and healthy as any similar number taken from any family record of the country.

BENJAMIN.

THE HOMESTEAD, LYSANDER TOWNSHIP, ONONDAGA COUNTY, NEW YORK

PART II.

THE HOLLAND ANCESTORS OF RULEF SCHENCK.

The ancestry of Roelof Martense Schenck, the first of the family in America, and from whom Rulef Schenck is traced in a following chapter, has been worked out, without a break, to the year 1346. The records of one or perhaps two generations are here missing, but thanks to the researches of van der Dussen, considerable information is at hand concerning the family as far back as 939, a brief outline of which has already been given.

It is our purpose here to trace the unbroken line of descent from 1346 to 1650, in the latter of which years Roelof Martense Schenck with his brother, Jan, and sister, Anetje, came to America.

In 1346, the head of the family was:—

1A. Heinrich Schenck van Nydeck, I., Knight, Lord of Afferden and Walbeck and Feoffer of Wachtendonk. He married Aleid van Rayde, heiress of Walbeck.

They had three children:—

 2A. I. Wynand, married Aleid van Bellinghoven, heiress of Walbrick. They had one son who died young, and the title and estates on Wynand's death, went to his brother, Heinrich (3A).

3A. II. Heinrich, see below.

4A. III. Lisbeth, a nun at Graevendael. Lisbeth died September 29, 1443.

3A. Heinrich Schenck van Nydeck, II., son of Heinrich (1A) and Aleid van Rayde, Knight, Lord of Afferden, Walbeck and Blyenbeck (the latter purchased by Wynand in 1405), Feoffer of Wachtendonk, married Alheid van Goen van Kaldenbrock, daughter of Allard, Lord van Kaldenbrock and Anna Monfoort. Heinrich died December 8, 1452.

They had three children:—

5A. I. Diederich. See below.

6A. II. Johann, Lord of Walbeck, Mayor of Middlelaer, 1491, married Inugard van Schonan. His son, Arnold, married Isabella van Oest, heiress of Hillenrath, and thus became the head of that branch of the family. Johann died May 24, 1491.

7A. III. Alheit, married Engelbert van Brempt, Mayor of Straden.

5A. Diederich Schenck van Nydeck, III., son of Heinrich (3A) and Alheid van Goen van Kaldenbrock, Lord of Afferden and Blyenbeck, Walbeck, and Arrsen, married Adelheit van Buren, daughter of Johann van Buren and Aleid van Arendahl. He died in August, 1487.

They had eleven children:—

8A. I. Winand, Lord of Arssen.

9A. II. Johann, Lord of Blyenbeck and Afferden.

10A. III. Roelmann, Lord of Walbeck.

11A. IV. Derick. See below.

12A. V. Heinrich, Lord of Horst.

13A. VI. Petronella, married Frederich van Huls.

14A. VII. Otto, monk at Leigburg.

15A. VIII.   Thomas, monk at Corneli Munster.
16A.   IX.   Alheid, nun at Grafenthal.
17A.   X.   Anna, nun at Grafenthal.
18A.   XI.   Lisbeth, nun in Gelden.

11A.   Derick Schenck van Nydeck, IV., son of Diederich (5A) and Adelheit van Buren, in the division of
his father's property received an estate in the Province
of Geldern, the estates of Nyfterich, Myllingen and
Loet and the court Ter Neirssan, near Hurst.   About
1515, after the death of his brothers, he became Lord
of Blyenbeck and Afferden.   He married Alheit Custers
of Arssen.

They had nine children:—
19A.   I.   Otto, died before 1485.
20A.   II.   Derick, born about 1485. See below.
21A.   III.   Peter, became Bailiff of Gibberfort.
22A.   IV.   Heinrich, born about 1490.
23A.   V.   Johann, born about 1495.
24A.   VI.   Winand, became a priest.
25A.   VII.   Adelheid.
26A. VIII.   Maria.
27A.   IX.   Margaretha.

20A.   Derick Schenck van Nydeck, V., son of Derick
(11A) and Alheit Custers, was born about 1485.   He
lived at Goch and was Lord of Afferden and Blyenbeck.
He married Maria van Galen.

They had one child:—
28A.   I.   Dederick, born about 1507.

28A.   Dederick Schenck van Nydeck, VI., son of
Derick (20A) and Maria van Galen, was born about
1507.   He was Lord of Afferden and Blyenbeck.   He
lived at Goch and married Anna van Berlaer.

They had five children:—

29A.   I. Martin, born at Goch, 1543, Knight. General in the Netherlands army, killed in a night attack upon the City of Nimeguen, August 11, 1589.

30A.   II. Peter, born 1547. See below.

31A. III. Johann, Colonel in the Spanish service.

32A.   IV. Maria Margaretha.

33A.   V. Maria Magdelina.

30A.   Peter Schenck van Nydeck, VII., son of Dederick (28A) and Anna van Berlaer, was born at Goch in 1547. He served with great distinction in the almost constant wars of his time, attaining the rank of General in the service of the Netherlands. He married at Doesburg, May 17, 1580, Johanna van Scherpenzeel.

They had two children:—

34A.   I. Wilhelmina.

35A.   II. Martin, born August 7, 1584.

35A.   Martin Schenck van Nydeck, VIII., son of Peter (30A) and Johanna van Scherpenzeel, was born at Doesburg, August 7, 1584. There is no record of his marriage.

He had three children:—

36A.   I. Roelof Martense, IX., born 1619. See American Ancestors of Rulef Schenck, p. 61.

37A.   II. Jan, born at Amersfoort; married at Flatlands, Long Island, Jannetje Stephens van Voorhees.

38A. III. Anetje, married at Flatlands, L. I., July 29, 1659, to Adrian Reyersz.

In 1650, these three children came to America. It is thought, but not absolutely proven, that they embarked from Holland on the ship "de Valckener," Wilheim Thomassen, Captain, sailing some time in March and landing in New Amsterdam June twenty-eighth. No record of the father, Martin, has been found in this country, but it is probable that he came with the family and being well advanced in years, may have died shortly after their arrival.

From Roelof and Jan, who had large families, there are many descendants now scattered throughout the United States. In addition to these families, there are also the descendants of Johannes Schenck, who at the age of 27 years, came with his wife, Maria Magdalena de Haes, to America in 1683. He resided for a time at New Amsterdam, Esopus (now Kingston) and Flatbush, and finally located permanently at Bushwick, Long Island.

The relationship between the descendants of Roelof and Jan on the one hand and those of Johannes on the other, may be accurately traced, as each family goes back to Derick Schenck van Nydeck and Alheit Custers. They had nine children, the second of whom was Derick and the third Peter. From Derick descended in the fourth generation Roelof and Jan; from Peter descended, also in the fourth generation, Johannes. The following diagram shows the relation of these two families.

There is no other family by the name for any long period in this country except one. In 1740, Michael Schenck emigrated from the Palatinate of the Rhine and located near Lancaster, Pa., and his descendants are fairly numerous in Pennsylvania, Virginia and North Carolina. They are of German and not Dutch extraction.

Roelof Martense Schenck (1a)—Neeltje Geretsen van Couwenhoven.

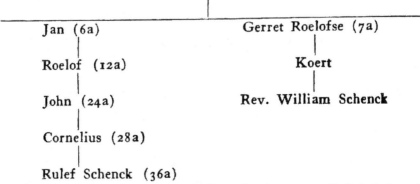

Jan (6a)

Roelof (12a)

John (24a)

Cornelius (28a)

Rulef Schenck (36a)

Gerret Roelofse (7a)

Koert

Rev. William Schenck

Diagram showing the relationship between Rulef Schenck and Rev. William Schenck, from the latter of whom is descended the Ohio branch of the family.

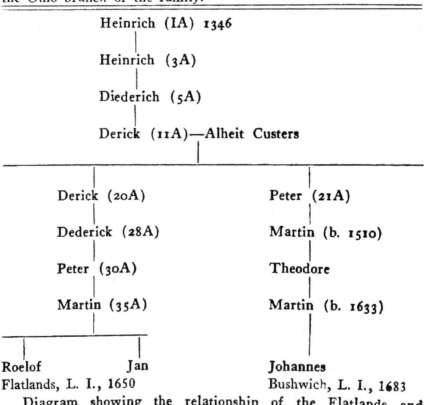

Heinrich (IA) 1346

Heinrich (3A)

Diederich (5A)

Derick (11A)—Alheit Custers

Derick (20A)

Dederick (28A)

Peter (30A)

Martin (35A)

Peter (21A)

Martin (b. 1510)

Theodore

Martin (b. 1633)

Roelof   Jan

Flatlands, L. I., 1650

Johannes

Bushwich, L. I., 1683

Diagram showing the relationship of the Flatlands and Bushwick branches of the Schenck family.

THE AMERICAN ANCESTORS OF RULEF SCHENCK.

1a. Roelof Martense Schenck, I., was born at Amersfoort, Holland, in 1619, and in 1650 came to New Amsterdam, settling at Flatlands, Long Island. In 1660, he married Neeltje Geretsen van Couwenhoven, daughter of Garret Wolphertson van Couwenhoven. She was born at Flatlands and baptized September 20, 1641.

They had six children:—

2a.   I. Martin, born at Flatlands, L. I., June 23, 1661; married June 20, 1686, Susanna Abrahamse Brinkerhoff; married, second, April 11, 1693, Elizabeth Minnen van Voorhees; married, third, Janetye van Voorhees. Martin was left the homestead farm and resided there until his death, May 2, 1721.

3a.   II. Anetje was born at Flatlands, L. I., about 1663 and June 10, 1681, married Jan Alberte Terhune. She died about 1685.

4a.   III. Jonica was born at Flatlands, L. I., about 1665 and June 7, 1684, married Peter Neefus.

5a.   IV. Marike was born at Flatlands, L. I., February 14, 1667, and February 15, 1687, married Isaac Hegeman.

6a.   V. Jan, born March 1, 1670. See p. 62.

7a.   VI. Gerret Roelofse was born at Flatlands, L. I., October 27, 1671, and 1693 married Neeltje Coerton van Voorhees, baptized December 5, 1680. He died at Pleasant Valley, Monmouth County, N. J., September 5, 1745. From Gerret Roelofse descended the Rev. William Schenck and the Ohio branch of the family.

Neeltje Geretsen (van Couwenhoven) Schenck died in 1673 and in 1675 Roelof Martense Schenck (1a) married Anetje Pieterse Wyckoff.

They had four children:—

8a.   VII.   Margaretta was born at Flatlands, L. I., January 16, 1668, and September 8, 1700, married Cornelius Willemse van Couwenhoven. She died at Middletown, N. J., December 16, 1751.

9a. VIII.   Neeltje was born at Flatlands, L. I., January 3, 1681, and about 1701 married Albert Willemse van Couwenhoven. She died at West Pleasant Valley, Monmouth County, N. J., July 7, 1751.

10a.   IX.   Mayke was born at Flatlands, L. I., January 27, 1684, and March 5, 1704, married Jan Lucase van Voorhees. She died at Flatlands, November 25, 1736.

11a.   X.   Sara was born at Flatlands, L. I., baptized December 18, 1685, and November 12, 1705, married Jacob Willemse van Couwenhoven. She died at Middletown, N. J., December 1, 1744.

Anetje Pieterse (Wyckoff) Schenck died and November 9, 1688, Roelof (1a) married Catryntyna Crigers. Roelof (1a) died in 1704. His will was probated August 3, 1705.

6a.   Jan Schenck, II., son of Roelof Martense (1a) and Neeltje Geretsen (van Couwenhoven) Schenck, was born at Flatlands, L. I., N. Y., March, 1670, and married Sara Willemse van Couwenhoven. She was born at Flatlands, L. I., December 27, 1674.

They had ten children.

12a.   I.   Roelof, born February 21, 1692. See p. 63.

13a.   II.   Peter.

14a. III. John, baptized in 1722.
15a. IV. Ann.
16a. V. Allchy.
17a. VI. Maria.
18a. VII. Sarah.
19a. VIII. Nellie.
20a. IX. Leah.
21a. X. Jane.

Jan Schenck (6a) died at Pleasant Valley, Monmouth County, N. J., January 30, 1753. Sara Willemse (van Couwenhoven) Schenck died January 31, 1761.

12a. Roelof Schenck, III., son of Jan (6a) and Sara Willemse (van Couwenhoven) Schenck, was born at Flatlands, Long Island, N. Y., February 21, 1692, and in 1716 married Geesie Hendrickson. She was born in October, 1696.

They had five children:

22a. I. Sarah was baptized in 1717 and married Joseph van Mater.
23a. II. Catherine was baptized in 1718 and married —— de Hart of Long Island.
24a. III. John, born January 22, 1720. See below.
25a. IV. Eleanor was baptized in 1725 and married Garret Conover.
26a. V. Hendrick was born in 1731; married Katherine Holmes; died August 21,. 1766.

Roelof Schenck (12a) died January 19, 1766. Geesie (Hendrickson) Schenck died September 20, 1747. They are buried at Pleasant Valley, N. J.

24a. John Schenck, IV., son of Roelof (12a) and Geesie (Hendrickson) Schenck, was born at Pleasant Valley, January 22, 1720, and November 26, 1741, married Jacamyntie van Couwenhoven.　She was born October 4, 1717.

They had four children:

27a.　　I.　Rulief was born July 21, 1742, and married Sarah Lippert.　They had three sons, Rulief (VI), Daniel and Moses.　About 1800 the family removed to Ohio, locating near Cincinnati.

28a.　　II.　Cornelius, born September 19, 1744.　See below.

29a.　　III.　Gasha was born September 14, 1748.　Married Aaron van Dorn.

John Schenck (24a) died June 27, 1749.

28a.　Cornelius Schenck, V., son of John (24a) and Jacamyntie (van Couwenhoven) Schenck, was born September 19, 1744, and July 3, 1765, married Margaret (Taylor), the widow of James Hankenson.　She was born in New Jersey, in November, 1742.

They had six children:

30a.　　I.　Eleanor was born July 11, 1766.

31a.　　II.　Gasha was born September 18, 1767.

32a.　　III.　John was born in New Jersey, April 7, 1770. He married Mary Quackenbush.　They had fourteen children.　He died January 8, 1850, at Springport, Cayuga County, N. Y.

33a.　　IV.　Mary was born March 29, 1772.

34a.　　V.　Margaret was born April 21, 1774.

35a.　　VI.　Rulef, born August 4, 1776.　See p. 65.

Cornelius Schenck (28a) died in January, 1790.

PART III.

THE DESCENDANTS OF RULEF SCHENCK

1. Rulef Schenck, VI. was born in Freehold, Monmouth Co., New Jersey, August 4, 1776. In 1802, he married Elsie Baird, daughter of William and Caroline Baird. She was born in Millstone, Somerset Co., N. J., March 8, 1785.

They had twelve children:

2 I. Sally, born February 2, 1803. See p. 66.

3 II. John, born June 12, 1804. See p. 67.

4 III. Catherine was born February 11, 1806, at Charleston, Montgomery County, New York. In 1815 she removed with the family to Onondaga County and lived on the Homestead in Lysander until the death of her parents. After the death of her mother in 1857, she resided with her sister Eliza in Plainville, Onondaga County, N. Y., where she died June 21, 1859. Catherine never married.

5 IV. Margaret, born August 26, 1807. See p. 70.

6 V. Benjamin Baird, born July 20, 1809. See p. 70.

7 VI. Eliza, born April 13, 1811. See p. 74.

8 VII. Son, unnamed, born June 17, 1813; died July 4, 1813.

9 VIII. Eleanor, born April 30, 1815. See p. 74.

10 IX. Hannah V——, born August 13, 1817. See p. 76.

11 X. William Baird, born November 5, 1819. See p. 78.

12 XI. James L., born May 25, 1823. See p. 79.

13 XII. Rulef, born October 23, 1827. See p. 80.

Rulef Schenck (1) died at the Homestead, near Plainville, N. Y., April 15, 1852. Elsie died at the same place five years later, November 3, 1857.

There were born of these parents twelve children, of whom one died in infancy and one at the age of 33 years. Of the other ten, Sally, Eliza, Eleanor and Hannah lived to be 80 or more years of age. The average age of the eleven children who lived to adult life, was 70 years, 1 month and 15 days.

SEVENTH GENERATION IN AMERICA.

2.   Sally Schenck, VII., daughter of Rulef (1) and Elsie (Baird) Schenck, was born at Charleston, Montgomery County, N. Y., February 2, 1803, and December 22, 1830, married Alfred Wilson,* son of William and Mary Wilson. He was born in Vermont, April 29, 1798.

They had nine children:

14 I.   Austin Wycoff, born October 18, 1821. See p. 80.

15 II.   Charlotte M., born February 25, 1824. See p. 81.

16 III.   Dennis Kennedy, born August 23, 1825. See p. 81.

17 IV.   Jane Ann, born July 23, 1827. See p. 81.

18 V.   Orinda M., was born November 17, 1830. She remained single and died at Plainville, N. Y., February 20, 1851.

19 VI.   Louisa A., born March 27, 1834. See p. 82.

*NOTE ON THE WILSON FAMILY.—William Wilson, the father of Alfred Wilson, was a preacher in the Christian Church. In 1806 he and his family removed from Vermont to the wilderness of Central New York. He located in Lysander Township and the little settlement which grew in the vicinity of his residence became known as Wilson's Corners. In 1821 a post office was established and the name was changed to Plainville.

SALLY SCHENCK WILSON

1803-1883

20 VII. James Alfred was born November 12, 1837. He remained on the homestead of his father and before attaining his majority came into possession of the farm by purchase, but owing to failing health, he relinquished the property and sought to regain his strength by a trip to Florida. He died at Jacksonville, Florida, January 8, 1858. James never married.

21 VIII. William H. was born June 15, 1840, and died Feb- 8, 1841.

22 IX. Francis A. was born June 28, 1842, and died May 28, 1845.

Alfred and Sally lived on the Wilson Farm in the Township of Lysander, Onondaga County, N. Y., until Alfred's death, which occurred February 4, 1854. Sally continued to reside there until April, 1868, when she removed to Meridian, Cayuga County, N. Y., where she made her home with her daughter, Charlotte, until July, 1882. She then removed to the home of her daughter, Jane Ann, dying there December 15, 1883.

3. John Schenck, VII., son of Rulef (1) and Elsie (Baird) Schenck, was born at Charleston, Montgomery County, N. Y., June 12, 1804, and October 13, 1830, married Perlina, daughter of Richard and Nancy Sullivan. (See pp. 68, 70 and 79.) She was born December 19, 1810.

They had seven children:

23 I. Elsie was born August 3, 1831, and died April 24, 1832.

24 II. Parna Eleanora, born September 2, 1833. See p. 82.

25 III. Harriet Livona, born September 12, 1836. See p. 83.

26 IV. James Harvey was born July 11, 1840, and died
February 5, 1843.

27 V. John Sullivan, born March 1, 1844. See p. 83.

28 VI. Nancy Theresa was born December 1, 1846, and
died May 19, 1851.

29 VII. Perlina Adele, born May 5, 1851. See p. 84.

Perlina (Sullivan) Schenck died June 6, 1851. John Schenck (3) married, July 21, 1852, Mrs. Parna Gorham, widow of Freeman Gorham, daughter of Richard* and Nancy Sullivan, and sister of his first wife.

They had one child:

30 I. Benjamin Freeman, born January 11, 1854. See p. 84.

Parna (Sullivan) Schenck died January 27, 1857. On September 7, 1858, John again married, taking for his third wife, Mrs. Julia Hall, who resided at Conquest, Cayuga County, N. Y. They had no children. Julia (Hall) Schenck died at Plainville, N. Y., April 19, 1880. John Schenck (3) died at Plainville, N. Y., May 3, 1884, and was buried in the village cemetery.

The following obituary, published at the time of John Schenck's death, gives a vivid picture of the man and his sterling character:

The community of Plainville has just been called to experience a common sorrow in the demise of Deacon John Schenck, who departed this life on Saturday last, after a week's illness. All the ministrations of the affectionate son and daughter-in-law, and of the skillful and worthy physician, were unavailing to restore health; and so we bow in sorrow to the inscrutable way and will of Providence.

*NOTE.—Richard Sullivan was a son of John and Sybal Sullivan and was born May 13, 1792. He was married August 19, 1809, to Nancy Faulkner, at Green, Chenango County, N. Y. Nancy (Faulkner) Sullivan was born October 11, 1790, and died February 14, 1850.

For sixty-nine years, John Schenck has been a worthy and respected citizen of the town of Lysander. Many important trusts were committed to his care, and his integrity remains unquestioned. In every question relating to the public good, he was actively and deeply interested. He was a modest man, and yet was fearless for and in the right. Keen perception, honest judgment, strong convictions, with moral courage, were among his characteristics as a parent, a citizen, and a man. He encouraged and assisted the young, helped the unfortunate, ministered to the poor, and sympathized with the sorrowing.

In 1842 he publicly professed loyalty to God, united with the Christian Church at Plainville, and remained an honored and respected member until called to "join the choir invisible."

Forty years of Christian service revealed the true character of the man. His faithfulness, self-sacrifice, and devotion to religion are well-known. He was a contented burden-bearer, counting it a pleasure to not only live but work for his God and Savior. Here he will be sadly missed, for his seat is empty. In social life, his presence was an inspiration and a welcome

Death of a Notable Man.

John Schenck, whose death at his home in Plainville is announced, had lived in the town of Lysander for a period of 69 years, during which time he had become widely and favorably known to a large class of citizens. The record he leaves is to his honor and glory. The ancestry from which Deacon Schenck sprung dated back to days of Charlemagne. His birth place was Charleston, Montgomery county, and the date of his birth June 12, 1804. At Charleston the first eleven years of his life were spent, with scant privileges, as far as education and enjoyment were concerned. In 1815 the family took up a residence in Lysander, then a howling wilderness, accessible from their former situation only by caravan over pathless wastes. Nine days were consumed in making the trip. How they succeeded in their endeavors let the well-cleared and finely-productive farms, now in possession of the family, testify.

On every question of interest to the public welfare he was deeply interested. In politics he was a staunch Republican, and only so because he loved his country, and thought that party the preserver of its liberties. He trusted his party implicitly with true devotion to its principles. He was a modest man, and yet he was fearless for and in the right. Keen perception, honest judgment, strong convictions and moral courage were his characteristics as a parent, man and citizen. He was thrice married, first to Perlina Sullivan, second Mrs. Parna Gorham and third

Standard May 10, 1884

His counsel was wise, his exemplary. He was every-lled "Uncle John" by all. nd confidence toward him,

Truly, our loss is great ve that that which is our more exceeding weight of f the Church and society kind Providence.

is late residence and also

The large gathering of the sincere sorrow of all. ife-long friend of the ae-to the personal request of vices, assisted by Rev. E. E. Good Templars presented mark of appreciation to and interested member of

26 IV. James Harvey was born July 11, 1840, and died February 5, 1843.

27 V. John Sullivan, born March 1, 1844. See p. 83.

28 VI. Nancy Theresa was born December 1, 1846, and died May 19, 1851.

29 VII. Perlina Adele, born May 5, 1851. See p. 84.

Perlina (Sullivan) Schenck died June 6, 1851. John Schenck (3) married, July 21, 1852, Mrs. Parna Gorham, widow of Freeman Gorham, daughter of Richard* and Nancy Sullivan, and sister of his first wife.

They had one child:

30 I. Benjamin Freeman, born January 11, 1854. See p. 84.

Parna (Sullivan) Schenck died January 27, 1857. On September 7, 1858, John again married, taking for his third wife, Mrs. Julia Hall, who resided at Conquest, Cayuga County, N. Y. They had no children. Julia (Hall) Schenck died at Plai—

John Schenck (3) died at

1884, and was buried in the

The following obituary,

Schenck's death, gives a v

his sterling character:

The community of Plainvill

ence a common sorrow in the

who departed this life on Satu

All the ministrations of the affe

and of the skillful and worth

restore health; and so we bow

and will of Providence.

*NOTE.—Richard Sullivan was

and was born May 13, 1792. H

Nancy Faulkner, at Green, Chen:

ner) Sullivan was born October 1

For sixty-nine years, John Schenck has been a worthy and respected citizen of the town of Lysander.   Many important trusts were committed to his care, and his integrity remains unquestioned. In every question relating to the public good, he was actively and deeply interested. He was a modest man, and yet was fearless for and in the right. Keen perception, honest judgment, strong convictions, with moral courage, were among his characteristics as a parent, a citizen, and a man. He encouraged and assisted the young, helped the unfortunate, ministered to the poor, and sympathized with the sorrowing.

In 1842 he publicly professed loyalty to God, united with the Christian Church at Plainville, and remained an honored and respected member until called to "join the choir invisible."

Forty years of Christian service revealed the true character of the man. His faithfulness, self-sacrifice, and devotion to religion are well-known. He was a contented burden-bearer, counting it a pleasure to not only live but work for his God and Savior. Here he will be sadly missed, for his seat is empty. In social life, his presence was an inspiration and a welcome addition to every circle of society. His counsel was wise, his influence great, his life, as a whole, exemplary. He was everybody's friend, and was familiarly called "Uncle John" by all. The young were attracted in love and confidence toward him, and the aged respected him, worthily. Truly, our loss is great in his death; but we confidently believe that that which is our affliction, works out for him a far more exceeding weight of glory. The united, sincere sorrow of the Church and society can only be healed by the grace of a kind Providence.

Funeral services were held at his late residence and also at the Church in Plainville, Tuesday. The large gathering of relatives and friends bore witness to the sincere sorrow of all. Rev. W. J. Grimes, of Memphis, a life-long friend of the deceased, was present, and in obedience to the personal request of the deceased, conducted the funeral services, assisted by Rev. E. E. Colburn, pastor of the Church. The Good Templars presented a beautiful floral pillow, as a slight mark of appreciation to the memory of one who was a true and interested member of their order.

Thus all that was mortal of our father, brother, friend, was laid in the house appointed for all living, to await God's call to life and love in eternity. The family of the deceased have the sympathy of all in their bereavement.   E. E. C.

5. Margaret Schenck, VII., daughter of Rulef (1) and Elsie (Baird) Schenck, was born at Charleston, Montgomery County, N. Y., August 26, 1807, and April 11, 1827, married Peter Bratt, son of John and Rebecca Bratt. He was born July 21, 1802.

They had five children:

31 I. Eliza Ann was born April 10, 1828, and died February 2, 1842.
32 II. John, born December 17, 1831. See p. 85.
33 III. Elsie, born September 19, 1833. See p. 85.
34 IV. Sarah Catherine, born July 12, 1838. See p. 86.
35 V. Peter Schenck, born February 7, 1846. See p. 86.

Peter Bratt died at Plainville, N. Y., April 14, 1874. Margaret (Schenck) Bratt (5) died at Plainville, January 31, 1875.

6. Benjamin Baird Schenck, VII., son of Rulef (1) and Elsie (Baird) Schenck, was born at Charleston, Montgomery County, N. Y., July 20, 1809, and June 21, 1838 married Harriet, daughter of Richard and Nancy Sullivan. (See pp. 67, 68 and 79). She was born near Cross Lake, in the Town of Lysander, Onondaga County, N. Y., January 10, 1817.

They had three children:

36 I. Benjamin Rush was born at Plainville, June 12, 1839. At the age of four years he was able to read and manifested a remarkable interest in nature and scientific facts. At the age of ten his father, who

MARGARET SCHENCK BRATT

1807-1875

were of the most interesting kind—full of life and

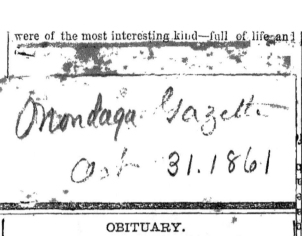

Onondaga Gazette
Oct 31. 1861

OBITUARY.

DIED—In Plainwell, Allegan County, Michigan, on the 14th of Sept. 1861, in the 23d year of his age, BENJ. RUSH SCHENCK, son of Dr. B. B. and HARRIET SCHENCK, of Plainville.

The subject of the above notice was the oldest of three children of B. B. and Harriet Schenck and was born in Plainville, N. Y., June 12th 1839. At the age of four years, he manifested a readiness of scientific attainments. His opportunities were those of a common or district School, eight or nine months of each year.

At ten years of age, he was found capable for the duties of the village Post Office, the which he pursued to the satisfaction of all parties, for nearly four years, treating every person with respect, nor was he ever remiss or negligent. His father, at that early age, divided with him the profits of the office, and it was found at the end of the 4th year, that he had accumulated a library of nearly fifty dollars' worth. They were of such interesting works as were advertised in the newspapers of the different parties. He had read these works and kn

was then postmaster, found him capable of doing the routine work of the office and divided the income with him. By his fourteenth year, Benjamin had accumulated a library, extensive for that period. Although he had but meager advantages in the way of education, he obtained a teacher's certificate at sixteen years of age and taught school in Van Buren. The following summer he attended the Monroe Collegiate Institute at Elbridge, N. Y., where he became the intimate friend of Professor Wilson. In 1856-57, he taught at Lysander, and the next year returned to the Institute at Elbridge. The winter of 1857 and 1858 he spent teaching a select school, held in the hall above the store of his father in Plainville.

Benjamin Rush, or Rush as he was called, then attended the Academy at Homer. In '59 and '60 he taught at Truxton, Cortland County, but he had to relinquish the school on account of failing health.

In the spring of 1861 he visited relatives in Michigan and Illinois and obtained a position to teach at Berrien, Michigan. In a letter sent to his home, he stated that "it was just the situation he had so earnestly longed for," but added that it seemed to him that he would never teach the school. While waiting for the term to open, he remained with his aunt, Hannah Schenck Fenner, at Plainwell. On the 3rd. of September he was taken ill and died September 14, 1862. He was interred at Plainville, N. Y.

Benjamin Rush Schenck possessed in a remarkable degree that intellectual superiority which overcomes surrounding obstacles, and which local seclusion cannot withhold from general appreciation.

37 II. Adrian Adelbert, born March 26, 1842. See p. 87.

38 III. Henrietta Maria, born November 10, 1843. See p. 91.

Benjamin Baird Schenck (6) died at Memphis, N.
Y., March 22, 1883. Harriet (Sullivan) Schenck died
at Memphis, February 2, 1899. They are buried in the
cemetery at Plainville.

Benjamin Baird Schenck, M. D., was the fifth child and the
second son of Rulef and Elsie Baird Schenck. When a lad of
six years, he removed with the family from Montgomery County
to Onondaga County and his early years were spent on the farm
which his father took up in Lysander Township. As he grew
to manhood, it became evident that physically he was not strong
enough for the strenuous life of the farm, and at the age of
twenty-three he entered the private school of T. W. Allis, in
Skaneateles, where he remained eighteen months, except for a
short interval during which he was engaged in teaching district
school. In 1834 he attended one term at the Homer Academy, and
the following spring began the study of medicine under Dr. Joseph
H. Skinner, of Plainville. In the winter of 1835 and 1836, he
attended lectures at the medical college at Fairfield, N. Y., and
his final course was pursued at the Geneva Medical College,
from which he received a diploma to practice February 10, 1835.
Soon after this he began practice in Plainville.

Not being satisfied with the science of regular medicine, as
taught and practiced at that time, Doctor Schenck took up the
subject of homeopathy and after several years of investigation
adopted it as his mode of practice.

In 1844 he united with the Christian Church of Plainville
and two years subsequently, June, 1846, at the Christian Conference in Dundee, he was admitted a member of that body and
given the credentials of "an ordained minister of the Gospel of
Jesus Christ." He was a close student of the Bible and spent
much of his time, not taken up with the activities of practice,
in searching the Scriptures. Four years after his ordination, a
conference of the Christian Church declared him "out of harmony with the church on account of his literal interpretation
of the Bible." He continued, however, for several years to
preach the doctrines he had imbued from his study of the Scrip-

BENJAMIN BAIRD SCH...
1809-1883

OBITUARY.

Benjamin Baird Schenck, M. D.

Died at Memphis, N. Y., Thursday, March 22, 1883, Benjamin Baird Schenck, M. D.

Benjamin Baird Schenck, M. D., was born in Charlestown, Montgomery county, N. Y., July 20, 1809. His father, Rulef Schenck, was of illustrious German descent. His ancestors emigrated to this country in 1640, and settled in Flatlands, New Jersey. Benjamin was the fifth child and second son, and at the age of six years came with his parents to Onondaga county, who settled in the town of Lysander, then a wilderness, in 1815. His early advantages for education were limited, his boyhood days being occupied in helping his father in clearing land and other farm duties.

Not until the age of twenty-three, when failing health showed his constitution unfitted for the then rough life of a farmer, did he turn his attention toward a profession. At that time he entered the private school of T. W. Allis, of Skaneateles, where he remained some eighteen months. In 1834 he attended one term at Homer Academy, then one of the flourishing schools of the State, and the following spring began the study of medicine in the office of Dr. J. H. Skinner, of Plainville, attending a course of lectures at the Medical College, at Fairfield. N. Y., in 1835—6, graduating February 10, 1838, at Geneva College. In June, 1838, he married Harriet, daughter of Captain R. Sullivan, of Seneca county, who survives him. In 1838 he began the practice of medicine in Plainville, which he continued, with intervals of rest, until 1876. In 1844 he united with the Christian Church; soon after was ordained a minister and preached frequently for many years.

Early in 1851, after thorough investigation, he adopted Homœopathy as his mode of practice, carrying with him into the new school all but two of his former patrons. From 1857 to 1864 he was engaged in mercantile pursuits, in the mean time teaching several terms of a select school. He held a lieutenant's commission in the State militia four years, a captain's seven, and was honorably discharged. In 1849 he was appointed postmaster at Plainville, held the office until Pierce's administration in 1853; was reappointed in 1863, and held the commission at his death. Always a Whig in politics he was quite active in his party's ranks until 1853, when the defeat of Scott and Graham took him out of active politics, since which time he continued a strong Republican in principal, though not participating in the matter of voting.

One Son, A. A. Schenck, of this city, and one daughter, Mrs. J. V. Norton, of Memphis, also survive him.

Funeral services will take place at Memphis Monday, March 26, at 10 a. m.

RESIDENCE OF DR. B. B. SCHENCK, PLAINVILLE, ONONDAGA COUNTY, N.Y.

B. B. Schrock

Benjamin Baird Schenck, M.D., was born in Charleston, Montgomery Co., N. Y., July 20, 1809. His father, Rulof Schenck, was of illustrious German descent. He settled in the northwest corner of this county, then a wilderness, in 1815.

Benjamin was the fifth child and second son. His early advantages for education were limited, his boyhood days being spent on a farm and in clearing land. At the age of twenty-three, his health failing, he entered the private school of T. W. Allis, at Skaneateles, where he remained eighteen months, with the exception of a short period spent in teaching district school. In 1834 he attended one term at Homer academy, and the following spring began the study of medicine, under Joseph H. Skinner, of Plainville, attending his first course of lectures at the medical college, Fairfield, N. Y., in 1835 and 1836. His final course was taken at Geneva college, where he graduated Feb. 10, 1838. The same year he began practice in Plainville. In 1844 he united with the Christian church of that place, and four years subsequently was ordained a minister by a conference of that body, and continued to preach till 1852. The conference that year, on account of his literal interpretation of the Scriptures, declared him "out of harmony with the church."

Meanwhile he had commenced an examination of homoeopathy, by reading Hahnemann's "Organon," and Hartmann's "Acute and Chronic Diseases." Continuing his investigations patiently through 1849 and 1850, he, early in 1851, adopted homoeopathy as his mode of practice, carrying with him into the new school all but two of his former patrons. In 1852 he took his brother-in-law, who for three years had been his student, into partnership with him, and in two years resigned in his favor.

Dr. Schenck then entered into mercantile business, but the crash of 1857 and the war of the rebellion seriously embarrassed him, so that he was induced to renew his practice, which since then has steadily increased.

In June, 1838, he married Harriet, daughter of Capt. R. Sullivan, of Seneca county. He held a lieutenant's commission in the State militia four years, and a captain's seven years, and was honorably discharged.

In 1849 he was appointed postmaster at Plainville, held the office till 1853, was reappointed in 1863, and still holds the office.

When young the doctor was prominent in church music, and only left the choir when he entered the pulpit, in June, 1846. He has had an unbroken residence in the school district where he resides since 1815, and was the first to start and teach a select school in the place.

tures. In 1862 he commenced the study of Greek and read most of the Bible in that language.

In 1852 he took his brother-in-law, Doctor Sullivan, who for three years had been his student, into partnership with him and two years later withdrew from practice to enter into mercantile business. He opened a general store in Plainville. The panic of 1857 and the Civil War seriously embarrassed him and he resumed practice. He was postmaster from 1849 to 1853, was reappointed in 1863 and held the office until he retired from business life. He held a lieutenant's commission in the State Militia for four years and a captain's for seven years. He continued to practice medicine until 1876, when he removed to Memphis, N. Y., to make his home with his daughter, Henrietta. While residing there his professional services were frequently sought, especially in consultation. He died at Memphis, March 22, 1883.

Dr. Benjamin Baird Schenck was untiring in his energy and industry. He was possessed of a genial disposition which won him many friends and was ever ready to help those in sorrow or in distress.

The following tribute to his memory was adopted by the Central New York Medical Society at a meeting held on September 20, 1883:

"Benjamin Baird Schenck, M. D., was among the earliest converts from the Old School to Homeopathy in the County of Onondaga, and was always faithful to its law in his treatment of the sick. He was an organic member of this society and almost always present at, and active in its meetings. He passed away from us on the 22nd. of March, 1883. In his death, we as a society, feel that we have lost one of our best.

"A man true in all the relations of life; skillful, modest, and sympathetic as a physician; patriotic and public-spirited as a citizen; and noble, just and true as a man; a Christian gentleman.

"As a society, we extend our sympathies to his family and friends in their loss.

WM. A. HAWLEY,
A. J. BREWSTER,
WM. M. GWYNN,
Committee."

7. Eliza Schenck, VII., daughter of Rulef (1) and Elsie (Baird) Schenck, was born in Charleston, Montgomery County, N. Y., April 13, 1811, and July 14, 1832, married Solomon B. Spaulding, son of Solomon and Mary Spaulding. He was born at Boston, Mass., January 27, 1808.

They had four children:

39 I.   Burns, born March 25, 1833. See p. 91.
40 II.   Mary C., born October 30, 1837. See p. 92.
41 III.   Annie Laura, born April 28, 1843. See p. 92.
42 IV.   Dealia, born February 2, 1850. See p. 92.

Solomon B. Spaulding died at Fulton, Oswego County, N. Y., June 11, 1881 and was buried at Plainville, N. Y. Eliza (Schenck) Spaulding (7) died at the home of her daughter, Mary C. Phelps, Fulton, N. Y., on February 27, 1895. The funeral was held at Fulton and burial took place at Plainville.

9. Eleanor Schenck, VII., daughter of Rulef (1) and Elsie (Baird) Schenck, was born in the Township of Lysander, Onondaga County, N. Y., April 30, 1815, and June 26, 1834, she married Frederick W. Fenner,* son

*NOTE ON THE FENNER FAMILY.—The History of the Fenner Family, compiled by Lucinda T. Fenner, of Plainwell, Mich., and published in 1908, gives in a very interesting manner the early history of this family.

Captain Arthur Fenner, the ancestor of Frederick W. and Russell B. Fenner, was born in England in 1622. He arrived at Providence, R. I., February 27, 1649, and until his death in 1703 lived about four miles from that city. His second son, Thomas, had eleven children, the sixth, Joseph, having been born in 1693. The latter had six children, the youngest of whom, born in 1737, was Asahel, who had two sons, James L. and Joseph.

James L. Fenner was born in Rhode Island in 1777. In 1801 he married Betsey Perry, a relative of Commodore Perry, the naval hero of the war of 1812. The spring following their marriage they moved to New York State, settling temporarily in the vicinity of Manlius, Onondaga County. In 1804 they located at Pompey, where James erected the first saw mill and was a partner in the first grist mills. During the residence in Pompey six children were born, the fourth being Frederick W., and the fifth, Russell B. Fenner. These brothers

ELEANOR SCHENCK FENNER
1815-1899

FREDERICK W. FENNER
1811-1876

of James L. and Betsey (Perry) Fenner. He was born September 9, 1811, at Pompey, Onondaga County, N. Y.

They had six children:

43 I. Frederick Byron was born February 7, 1835, and died May 30, 1836.

44 II. James Rulef, born August 12, 1836. See p. 93.

45 III. Avis Melissa, born in Lysander, N. Y., June 6, 1839.

46 IV. Sarah Ellen, born September 3, 1841. See p. 93.

47 V. Frederick William, born June 11, 1847. See p. 94.

48 VI. Franklin Eddy was born in Lysander, April 15, 1853, and died April 10, 1857.

Frederick W. Fenner died near Jacksonville, N. Y., February 24, 1876. Eleanor (Schenck) Fenner (9) married December 12, 1878, Perry Hazard Hinsdell, of the Township of Salina, Onondaga County, N. Y.; he was born April 21, 1820, and died at Syracuse, N. Y., March 12, 1907.

Eleanor (Schenck Fenner) Hinsdell (9), died December 31, 1899, and was buried beside her first husband at Jacksonville, N. Y. An obituary notice pubished at the time of her death is as follows:

were of the sixth generation in America.

In 1818 the family removed to Lysander, Onondaga County, N. Y., where James L. died January 16, 1851. Three of the sons, Darius P., Russell B., and Luther, removed to Michigan, the former in 1840, the two latter in 1844.

Frederick W. Fenner, the fourth son of James L. and Betsey Perry Fenner, removed from Pompey to Lysander, with the others of the family, when six years of age. It has been said of him: He was an earnest advocate of reform and a prominent temperance worker, alive to all educational progress. His opportunities for attending school were limited, but being a great reader and thinker, he kept pace with the times, although he was a busy, hardworking farmer. He taught school when eighteen years of age with success, and also taught several terms after he was married. He was the first town superintendent of schools appointed by the governor. Whatever office he held, he was conscientious in administering for the public good and not for self-interest or gain. He was a friend to the needy. He was a fluent speaker and his impromptu speeches would do credit to those who have the present opportunities. *History of the Fenner Family.*

Eleanor Schenck Fenner Hinsdell entered into rest December 31, 1899.

In the passing of "Aunt Ellen" from this life, disappears the last of the generation, and the last of the household of one of the pioneers of Lysander Township.

In March, 1815, Rulef Schenck and his wife Elsie Baird Schenck, with their six children left Charleston, Montgomery County, N. Y., and journeyed in a wagon train to Lysander, Onondaga County, N. Y., to take up their abode in a log house which had been built for them in the wilderness.

Soon after their arrival Eleanor was born and grew to womanhood on the farm, doing her share of the household duties as she grew into them, which in those days were very arduous, as all the cloth for the garments worn by the family had to be spun and woven in the home. As she grew to womanhood she developed traits of character that were a blessing to all with whom she came in contact in after life—"in her mouth was the law of kindness," and she always had in mind the comfort and happiness of others.

In June, 1834, at the age of nineteen, she married Frederick W. Fenner, of the town of Pompey and their married life was one of continued harmony for forty-two years, when her husband passed away. They had six children, two of whom died in infancy.

She was again united in marriage December 12, 1878, to Perry H. Hinsdell, of North Syracuse. While young her educational advantages were limited, yet she was always well informed on the leading questions of her day, and her society was sought after by many friends and greatly enjoyed.

If to have been a loving and dutiful wife, an affectionate mother, a hospitable, charitable, and generous neighbor, and to have lived a consistent Christian all the years of her life, may it not be worthily said of her—"Well done, good and faithful servant, enter now into the joy of thy Lord."

10. Hannah V. Schenck, VII., daughter of Rulef (1) and Elsie (Baird) Schenck, was born in the Township of Lysander, Onondaga County, N. Y., August 13, 1817,

HANNAH SCHENCK FENNER

1817-1898

and September 28, 1837, married Russell B. Fenner, son of James L. and Betsey (Perry) Fenner and brother of Frederick W. Fenner. (See p. 74). He was born at Pompey, N. Y., February 9, 1814.

They had five children:—

49 I. Byron Russell, born March 4, 1839. See p. 95 .

50 II. Eliza Eleanor, born April 1, 1842. See p. 95.

51 III. William Perry, born December 22, 1844. See p. 96.

52 IV. Rulef James, born September 17, 1850. See p. 96.

53 V. Franklin Monroe, born October 11, 1854. See p. 97.

Russell B. and Hannah (Schenck) Fenner (10) removed from Onondaga County to Martin, Allegan County, Michigan, in 1844. He died March 27, 1896, and Hannah (Schenck) Fenner (10), April 25, 1898.

Russell B. Fenner grew up to manhood in Lysander Township, N. Y. Seven years after his marriage to Hannah Schenck they removed to Michigan, arriving in Martin, Allegan County, October 10, 1844. The History of the Fenner Family says of them: The appearance of the country was anything but inviting to the young couple who had left parents, brothers, sisters, and the friends of their youth in a well-settled neighborhood, to seek a home in the unbroken wilderness. He at once began cutting logs with which to build a house, succeeding so well that they were able to live in it that winter. He spent the winter in chopping off the timber for the purpose of clearing his farm.

There were many Indians in the country at that time, and they often came for him to take his dog and go with them to catch the deer which they had wounded. The squaws sometimes came to the house with their baskets, trading them with Mrs. Fenner for salt pork, flour, or such eatables as she had. The Indians often wanted to stay all night, and frequently they were allowed to roll up in their blankets and sleep beside the kitchen fire.

Three sons were added to the family after their removal to Michigan: Perry, James and Franklin. The earliest recollections of these boys are those of an almost unbroken wilderness, dotted here and there with small clearings upon which were built log houses and barns. In many cases the clearings were enclosed with brush fences, as was also the heavily timbered land, which was a range for all the stock of the neighborhood as well as deer and other wild animals in plenty. Some of the finest farms and farm buildings in the state are now upon that land.

To the older boys of the family fell the task of hunting the cows in the woods. To boys of today that would be a hard task, but they rather enjoyed it, especially when they found a sleek deer with the cows, as they often did. It was one of their chief means of excitement.

At this time very few of the roads were on section lines, as they now are, but ran angling through the woods, around big trees and swampy places.

After living in Martin nine years, Mr. Fenner moved to North Gunplain. There he bought eighty acres of land and built a commodious farmhouse and barns upon it. He was a man who was gifted in many respects. He had a keen insight into human nature which enabled him to make many friends. His farm and stock showed thrift and good management. Besides his interest in agricultural pursuits he was deeply interested in medical science, which he studied with much success, many times curing or helping sick people whom the doctors had given up. He was always active in promoting the intellectual advancement of the young. When meetings were held in the schoolhouse near his home, he and his wife contributed largely to their success, aiding in the singing and by their kindly, friendly manners encouraging others to help.

Genial and social in his nature, he always delighted to welcome a large circle of relatives and friends to his pleasant home. It was a delightful custom for many years before his death to have the children, grandchildren, and other relatives gather there on his birthday. Those occasions will long be remembered by the participants. On September 28, 1887, he and his wife celebrated the fiftieth anniversary of their marriage with a golden wedding. Relatives came from the East and West to add their gifts and join with their children, children's children, and other relatives, in making the day a memorable one to all who were present, as well as to the honored couple who had walked side by side for fifty years.

A few years before his death he bought a pleasant place in the village of Plainwell, still retaining his farm. For a few years after this he still retained mental and physical vigor remarkable for one of his years, but gradually his health failed, and he died March 27, 1896, survived by his wife and five chidren.

11. William Baird Schenck, VII., son of Rulef (1) and Elsie (Baird) Schenck, was born in the Township of Lysander, Onondaga County, N. Y., November 5, 1819, and January 12, 1843, married Catherine M. Vanderveer,

CATHERINE VANDERVEER SCHENCK
1822-1903

WILLIAM BAIRD SCHENCK
1819-1853

Obituary.

James L. Schenck, son of Rulef and Elsie Schenck, was born in the town of Lysander, Onondaga county, N. Y., on the 25th day of May, 1823. Receiving a fair education at the district and select schools in his native town, he devoted a portion of the time during his early manhood to teaching and farming. He was first married to Anna Tator, September 15, 1847. She died the following February. He married N. Maria Sullivan December 31, 1850, who, with their daughter, Mrs. Edgar Pomeroy, survive him. He was for many years an active member of Mohegan Lodge of Old Fellows, Seneca River Lodge F. & A. M., at Baldwinsville, N. Y., and later a member of the Chapter Lodge at said place. He was for some time connected with the State militia, and held a captain's commission in the cavalry branch of the service under Brigadier-General John A. Green.

In 1870 he removed to Syracuse and engaged in the hardware trade, which proving unsuccessful he closed it out and for a few years represented the Williams Mower and Reaper company, and later the Bradley Manufacturing company's agricultural implements in Minnesota and other Western States. Since severing his connection with the last named company he was not engaged in any extended business enterprises. For the past two or three years he has been somewhat out of health, and three weeks prior to his death he received a partial stroke of paralysis from which he partially rallied, but complications heart disease set in and he died at his home, 204 Grape-st., in this city, at 7:30 p. m., the 12th inst.

The surviving friends are comforted with the knowledge that he died with a Christian's hope. He died quietly, without a struggle.

Funeral services will be held at the house at 2 p. m., Friday. Interment at Plainville, Saturday.

JAMES L. SCHENCK

1823-1886

daughter of Garret and Ann Vanderveer. She was born at Florida, Montgomery County, N. Y., December 31, 1822.

They had three children:

    54 I.   Hulbert Luke, born December 6, 1843. See p. 97.

    55 II. Irwin Vanderveer, born November 2, 1846. See p. 98.

    56 III. James Shuler, born August 19, 1851. See p. 98.

William Baird Schenck (11) died in Lysander Township, March 17, 1853. Catherine (Vanderveer) Schenck died on the "William Baird Farm," March 3, 1903.

12.   James L. Schenck, VII., son of Rulef (1) and Elsie (Baird) Schenck, was born in the Township of Lysander, Onondaga County, N. Y., May 25, 1823, and September 15, 1847, married Ann Tator, daughter of Frederick I. and Polly Tator. (See note on page 81). She was born in the Township of Lysander. They had no children. Ann (Tator) Schenck died February 18, 1848. On December 31, 1850, James L. married Nancy Maria Sullivan, daughter of Richard and Nancy Sullivan. (See pages 67 and 68). She was born September 27, 1823.

They had two children:

    57 I. James Warren was born at Plainville, N. Y., May 12, 1854, and died at the home of his parents on Geddes Street, Syracuse, N. Y., November 24, 1883. He never married.

    58 II. Lelia Maria, born November 8, 1856. See p. 98.

James L. Schenck (12) died at his home, 204 Grape Street, Syracuse, N. Y., January 16, 1886. Nancy (Sullivan) Schenck died at Syracuse, July 1, 1906. They are both buried at Plainville.

13.   Rulef Schenck, VII., son of Rulef (1) and Elsie
(Baird) Schenck was born in Lysander Township, Onondaga County, N. Y., October 23, 1827, and February 27,
1850, married Emerancy Jane Emerick, daughter of
Abraham and Hannah Emerick.   She was born in Lysander Township, August 6, 1831.

They had three children:

  59 I.   Alice Maladine, born at the Homestead, Lysander
          Township, June 12, 1851.   Address, Plainville,
          N. Y.
  60 II. Effie Isadore, born February 12, 1854. See p. 99.
  61 III. William Baird, born July 21, 1859. See p. 99.

In 1883, Rulef Schenck (13) removed to the residence
of his brother, Dr. Benjamin Baird Schenck (6) in
Plainville and resided there until his death, June 28,
1888.   Emerancy (Emerick) Schenck died at the same
place October 20, 1905.   Both are buried in the cemetery at Plainville.

EIGHTH GENERATION IN AMERICA.

14.   Austin Wycoff Wilson, VIII., son of Alfred and
Sally (Schenck) Wilson (2) was born in Lysander, N.
Y., October 18, 1821, and February 2, 1843, married
Mary Ann Verity, daughter of James G. and Eunice
Verity.   She was born April 2, 1823.

They had one child:

  62 I.   Mervin James, born May 5, 1850. See p. 100.

Mary (Verity) Wilson died June 28, 1851, and January 13, 1853, Austin W. Wilson (14) married Mrs.
Eunice Snow.   They had no children.   Austin died at
Plainville, N. Y., April 3, 1858.   Eunice (Snow) Wilson
died March 10, 1889.

RULEF SCHENCK
1827-1888

RESIDENCE OF BENJAMIN BAIRD SCHENCK

15. Charlotte M. Wilson, VIII., daughter of Alfred and Sally (Schenck) Wilson (2), was born February 25, 1824, and February 6, 1842, married Jehial E. Tator, son of Frederick I. and Polly Tator. (See note below). He was born at Lysander, N. Y., November 14, 1820, and died November 30, 1884. Charlotte M. (Wilson) Tator married June 28, 1892, Samuel Wells. He died September 20, 1895, and Charlotte M. (Wilson, Tator) Wells married December 21, 1898, Benjamin Coats. Charlotte died at Meridian, Cayuga County, N. Y., May 1, 1907. Benjamin Coats died September 12, 1910.

16. Dennis Kennedy Wilson, VIII., son of Alfred and Sally (Schenck) Wilson (2), was born August 23, 1825, and October 29, 1846, married Lydia Amanda Tator, daughter of Frederick I. and Polly Tator. (See note below). She was born October 19, 1826.

They had one child:

63 I. Orinda More, born November 23, 1850. See p. 100.

Lydia Amanda (Tator) Wilson died February 1, 1854, and March 4, 1857, Dennis Kennedy Wilson (16) married Louisa B. Irish. They had no children. Dennis died July 5, 1865 and Louisa married in 1867, John Hunt. She died in November, 1868.

17. Jane Ann Wilson, VIII., daughter of Alfred and Sally (Schenck) Wilson (2), was born July 23, 1827, and February 5, 1847, married James M. Tator* son of

---

*NOTE.—It will be noticed that the first wife of James L. Schenck (12), the first husband of Charlotte M. Wilson (15), the wife of Dennis Kennedy Wilson (16) and the husband of Jane Ann Wilson (17) were brothers and sisters.

Frederick I. and Polly Tator. He was born at Lysander, N. Y., December 16, 1824.

They had two children:

> 64 I.   Anna Hubble, born September 7, 1849. See p. 101.
> 65 II.   Willard Jehial was born May 8, 1857, and died January 18, 1870.

James M. Tator died November 28, 1901. Jane Ann (Wilson) Tator (17). Address, R. F. D., Memphis, N. Y.

19.   Louisa A. Wilson, VIII., daughter of Alfred and Sally (Schenck) Wilson (2), was born March 27, 1834, and August 24, 1853, married Samuel W. Bates, son of James and Deborah Bates. They had no children.

Louisa A. (Wilson) Bates (19) died December 28, 1854.

24.   Parna Eleanora Schenck, VIII., daughter of John (3) and Perlina (Sullivan) Schenck, was born September 2, 1833, and February 1, 1854, married James Leslie Voorhees, son of James L. and Martha Voorhees. He was born at Whig Hill, near Plainville, N. Y., December 1, 1831.

They had four children:

> 66 I.   Martha Northrop was born October 3, 1854, and died November 19, 1871.
> 67 II.   John Schenck, born August 11, 1856. See p. 101.
> 68 III.   James Hubbell was born December 23, 1860, and died January 13, 1861.
> 69 IV.   Henry Peter, born December 1, 1861. See p. 101.

Parna (Schenck) Voorhees (24) died June 17, 1865. James Leslie Voorhees married April 10, 1867, Sarah Catherine Bratt (34). See p. 86.

25. Harriet Livona Schenck, VIII., daughter of John (3) and Perlina (Sullivan) Schenck, was born September 12, 1836, and October 2, 1853, married James S. Vedder, son of Aaron F. and Nancy Vedder. He was born at Lysander, N. Y., July 23, 1828. Soon after their marriage, they removed to Carrollton, Greene County, Ill., where they remained until 1872. They then removed to Washington, Kansas.

They had four children:

70 I. Inez Ann, born July 25, 1854. See p. 101.
71 II. Harriet Elnora, born December 1, 1856. See p. 102.
72 III. Lyman Norton, born November 27, 1858. See p. 103.
73 IV. Jennie Leslie was born at Carrollton, Ill., December 9, 1862, and died at Washington, Kan., October 18, 1873.

James S. Vedder was successively Register of Deeds, Tax Collector, Clerk of Courts and Sheriff of Greene County, Ill., and was for three terms Mayor of Washington, Kansas, as well as Postmaster, a position which he held at the time of his death, November 12, 1888. Harriet Livona (Schenck) Vedder: Address, Ventura, Cal.

27. John Sullivan Schenck, VIII., son of John (3) and Perlina (Sullivan) Schenck, was born at Plainville, N. Y., March 1, 1844, and January 3, 1865, married Jane Leslie Tomlinson, daughter of John H. and Harriet Tomlinson, and niece of James Leslie Voorhees. (See p. 82). She was born at Plainville, N. Y., January 5, 1845. They had no children. Jane (Tomlinson) Schenck died November 12, 1865, and March 1, 1866, John married Adaline Day, daughter of Hezekiah and Eliza Ann Day. (See p. 94.) She was born at Little Utica, N. Y., May 13, 1845.

They had one child:

74 I.   Floyd Sullivan, born September 21, 1874. See p. 103.

Adaline (Day) Schenck died near Plainville, N. Y., November 25, 1908, and June 12, 1910, John Sullivan Schenck (27), married Mrs. Sarah C. Winchel, daughter of Richard and Frances (Cogswell) Smith. She was born at Lysander, N. Y., September 23, 1833. John Sullivan Schenck (27): Address, Lysander, N. Y.

29. Perlina Adele Schenck, VIII., daughter of John (3) and Perlina (Sullivan) Schenck, was born May 5, 1851, and January 25, 1874, married at Washington, Kansas, Charles Smith, son of Stevens and Sophia C. Smith. He was born at Gorham, Cumberland County, Me., August 29, 1845.

They had five children:

75 I.   Charles Fred, born December 12, 1874. See p. 104.
76 II.   Nellie Leslie, born January 27, 1876. See p. 104.
77 III. Joseph Lowe, born November 23, 1877. See p. 105.
78 IV.   Harry James, born September 30, 1883. See p. 105.
79 V.   Harriet Marie, born May 16, 1885. See p. 105.

Perlina Adele (Schenck) Smith: Address, Washington, Kansas.

30. Benjamin Freeman Schenck, VIII., son of John (3) and Parna (Sullivan, Gorham) Schenck, was born at Plainville, N. Y., January 11, 1854, and December 31, 1874, married Ella Eliza Chittenden, daughter of Samuel Mallory and Julia Eliza (Parish) Chittenden. She was born at Baldwinsville, N. Y., December 24, 1854.

They had three children:—

80 I. Julia was born at Plainville, N. Y., January 1,
1877, and died January 14, 1877.

81 II. Lisle John, born June 10, 1879. See p. 106.

82 III. Elsie May, born May 7, 1881. See p. 106.

Benjamin Freeman Schenck (30) died at Plainville,
March 13, 1906. Ella Eliza (Chittenden) Schenck:
Address, Plainville, N. Y.

32. John Bratt, VIII., son of Peter and Margaret
(Schenck) Bratt (5), was born December 17, 1831, and
March 7, 1854, married Matilda Wilson, daughter of
William and Hannah Wilson (William Wilson was a
brother of Alfred Wilson, husband of Sally (Schenck)
Wilson (2)). Matilda (Wilson) Bratt was born at
Plainville, N. Y., June 13, 1832.

They had seven children:—

83 I. Frank Leslie, born November 1, 1857. See p. 106.

84 II. Charles Willis, born May 31, 1859. See p. 107.

85 III. Ella May, born September 21, 1862. See p. 107.

86 IV. Anna Isabell, born August 9, 1864. See p. 108.

87 V. Alice Merriman, born September 11, 1866. See
p. 108.

88 VI. Ernest Wilson, born December 26, 1869. See p. 109.

89 VII. Sarah Elsie, born November 12, 1872. See p. 109.

John Bratt (32) died at Baldwinsville, N. Y., April
11, 1902. Matilda (Wilson) Bratt died at Baldwinsville, N. Y., November 26, 1898. They are both buried
in the cemetery at Plainville, N. Y.

33. Elsie Bratt, VIII., daughter of Peter and Margaret (Schenck) Bratt (5), was born September 19, 1833,
and January 16, 1851, married Chauncey Hubbard, son
of Elijah and Eliza Hubbard. He was born in Albany
County, N. Y., November 19, 1826.

They had one child:—

    90 1. Ella Lillian, born December 31, 1854. See p. 109.

Elsie (Bratt) Hubbard (33) died at Plainville, N. Y., September 12, 1879. Chauncey Hubbard died at the same place, July 4, 1906.

34. Sarah Catherine Bratt*, VIII., daughter of Peter and Margaret (Schenck) Bratt (5), was born July 12, 1838, and April 10, 1867, married James Leslie Voorhees. (See p. 82).

They had six children:—

    91 I. Leslie Eleanora, born January 12, 1870.

    92 II. Sophia, born October 11, 1872. Graduated at Wellesley College in 1895, and received the degree of M. A. at the University of Michigan in 1910.

    93 III. James Leslie was born June 1, 1874, and died March 8, 1875.

    94 IV. Margaret was born July 5, 1877, and died February 13, 1889.

    95 V. Martha, born November 3, 1878. Graduated from Wellesley College in 1903.

    96 VI. James Leslie, 3rd, born September 8, 1880. Address, Reno, Nev.

Sarah Catherine (Bratt) Voorhees (34) died at Baldwinsville, N. Y., June 1, 1905. James Leslie Voorhees: Address, Baldwinsville, N. Y.

35. Peter Schenck Bratt, VIII., son of Peter and Margaret (Schenck) Bratt (5), was born February 7, 1846, and March 15, 1869, married Marta Nettie Carpenter, daughter of George and Ruth Carpenter. She was born in the Township of Granby, Oswego County, N. Y., June 3, 1848.

---

*Sarah Catherine retained the original spelling of her name, i. e., *Bradt*. While this is undoubtedly correct, it is here given *Bratt*, in order to retain uniformity.

They had seven children:—

97 I. Herbert Eugene, born February 13, 1870. See p. 110.
98 II. LeRoy, born July 23, 1872. See p. 110.
99 III. Arthur, born February 28, 1874. See p. 111.
100 IV. William Peter, born December 17, 1882. See p. 111.
101 V. Harry, born August 26, 1884. See p. 111.
102 VI. Raymond, born August 24, 1888. See p. 112.
103 VII. Ruth, born September 14, 1891. Address, 251 Fitch St., Syracuse, N. Y.

Peter Schenck Bratt (35) died January 13, 1904. Marta Nettie (Carpenter) Bratt died at Jordan, N. Y., May 3, 1906. They are buried in the Plainville cemetery.

37. Adrian Adelbert Schenck, VIII., son of Benjamin Baird (6) and Harriet (Sullivan) Schenck, was born at Plainville, N. Y., March 26, 1842, and married October 23, 1866, Harriet Parthenia Robinson, daughter of Horatio N. Robinson, A. M., LL. D., and Emma R. (Tyler) Robinson. She was born at Cincinnati, O., September 29, 1845.

They had three children:—

104 I. Elsie, born at Syracuse, N. Y., September 26, 1867.
105 II. Benjamin Robinson, born August 19, 1872. See p. 112.
106 III. Frederick Tyler was born at Syracuse, N. Y., March 21, 1878, and died March 25, 1878.

Adrian Adelbert Schenck (37) died at Syracuse, N. Y., February 25, 1909, and is buried at Oakwood Cemetery in Syracuse.

Adrian Adelbert Schenck was born in Plainville, N. Y., March 26, 1842. His education was obtained at the Monroe Collegiate Institute, at Elbridge, N. Y., which at that time was an academy of very considerable reputation.   After leaving Elbridge he went to Syracuse in 1864, entering the office of the Provost Marshal, where he remained until obtaining a position in 1865, in the canal office.

The next ten years were devoted to work in the offices of the Internal Revenue Service and County Clerk of Onondaga County. From 1876 to 1880 he held the important position of clerk of the courts.   In 1880 he returned to the Revenue Service, being Deputy Collector of Internal Revenue for the Twenty-fifth District. This position he held until the election of Cleveland to the Presidency in 1887, when he resigned.   During the sessions of the New York Legislature of 1888 and 1889, he was clerk of the Committee on Cities of the Senate, spending four days each week in Albany.   During these years he was prominent in politics in the Republican party, in whose tenets he was an uncompromising believer throughout his whole life.

On October 6, 1888, he was instrumental in the organization of the Engelberg Huller Company, becoming its first secretary and general manager, a position which he held continuously until his death, a period of over twenty-three years.   The success which attended this organization was largely due to his efforts and he was rewarded by seeing it grow into one of the most stable and prosperous of the manufacturing industries of Syracuse.

After the marriage of Mr. Schenck and Harriet P. Robinson, a daughter of Horatio N. Robinson, LL. D., in 1866, they resided on Montgomery Street until May, 1869, when they removed to a residence which they built at No. 8 Holland Street.   In 1894 a second home was built at 615 Park Avenue.

Mr. Schenck was a member of the Central City Lodge No. 305, F. and A. M., of the Royal Arcanum and many other organizations.   He was much interested in manufacturing and industrial questions and in 1907 and 1908 was the vice-president for the State of New York of the National Association of Manufacturers, the Board of Directors of which passed the following resolution:

At a regular meeting of the Board of Directors of the National Association of Manufacturers, held at Niagara Falls, New York, on July 16th, 1909, the following minute was unanimously adopted and spread upon the records:

Resolved: That in the death of our honored Vice-President for the State of New York, Mr. Adrian A. Schenck, the association sustains a severe and deplorable loss.

The elevation of Mr. Schenck to the Vice-Presidency having taken place at the instance of the delegates of his State at the annual convention of 1907 and his re-election following, gave abundant evidence of his popularity with his fellow members. The performance of his official duties during his term of office was such as to win for him the approval and admiration of his fellow members of the Board of Directors.

As a man of excellent judgment and unblemished character in his private and business affairs, he won the sincere affection and regard of all whose pleasure it was to know him.

We shall cherish his memory and the recollection of his virtues and the inspiration of his example will remain as a stimulus to others in the pursuit of lofty ideals and worthy achievements.

And we extend to his sorrowing family this token of our high regard for him whose loss to them, to us and to mankind at large is felt with deep affliction.

J. KIRBY, JR., *Pres't.*
GEO. T. BONDINOT, *Sec'y.*

Committee:
    LUDWIG DESSEN,
    C. C. HANCH,
    ENOS PAULLIN.

During May, 1908, Mr. Schenck's health failed, but he was able to attend to his business affairs until the day of his death, the 25th. day of February, 1909.

The gentleness of his character, combined with his high ideals, lifted him above the petty trials of every-day life, seeming to cause him to radiate good cheer, helpfulness and optimism wherever he went. To him no one ever appealed for help in vain. He lived for others and died mourned by a host of sincere friends. The esteem in which he was held by his intimate business associates is attested in the following:

At a meeting of the Board of Directors of the Engelberg Huller Company, held Monday, March 1st, at their office in Fayette Street, the following preamble and resolutions relative to the death of their late Secretary and Treasurer, Mr. A. A. Schenck, were presented and approved:

Whereas, For the fourth time during the history of this Company, we are called upon to mourn and record the death of a Director; and, in the death of our co-worker, Secretary, Treasurer, and friend, we have lost the greatest of them all; for while others had different interests, Mr. Schenck gave twenty of the best years of his life, with undivided devotion to the welfare of this organization. During all this time he worked for its interests and battled for its success. We alone know of its success and that no one has done more to achieve it, and we alone can measure our loss. As time has gone on we have learned to respect and love him and as time goes on we shall miss him more. Our loss and sorrow can only be exceeded by that of his family. Therefore, as an evidence of our appreciation and respect be it

Resolved, That his chair as Director remain unfilled; that a copy of this tribute be engraved, signed by the Board and presented to his family, and these proceedings recorded in the books of this Company and its purport be published in the daily papers.

J. R. MONTAGUE   JOHN E. SWEET
J. P. CROWELL   C. P. REMORE
C. E. HUTCHINSON   W. C. LIPE
            F. P. FELL

DEATH OF J. V. NORTON.

Startling and Unexpected Intelligence of his Death in Rio de Janeiro, Brazil, of Yellow Fever—A Sketch of his History, and Events Connected with his Visit to Brazil and Sudden Death.

We are pained to announce the death of Mr. John V. Norton, of Memphis, in this county, which occurred in the city of Rio de Janeiro, Brazil, on the 11th of February last. Mr. A. A. Schenck, brother-in-law of Mr. Norton, was informed this morning by Mr. Charles A. Sweet, that Mr. D. Valentine had received a letter from Mr. Ford, who has charge of a railway running from the city of Rio to a place called Regurda, some 150 miles back in the country, enclosing a letter addressed to J. H. Norton, esq., of Plainville, a brother of the deceased, and stating to Mr. Valentine that the letter must be delivered to Mr. J. H. Norton in person, and to no one else. Mr. V. wrote to Mr. J. H. Norton the fact of his having such a letter for him. Both Mr. Sweet and Mr. Schenck, knowing that the deceased was engaged in business in the city of Rio de Janeiro, and the communication being from Mr. Ford at Regurda, had hopes, though faint, all day that the communication might prove to be one of urgent business matters, but feared the worst. Mr. J. H. Norton arrived in town by the 7 P. M. train on the Oswego and Syracuse road and was met at the depot by Mr. Schenck, when they proceeded to the store of Mr. Valentine, where the letter was delivered, and which confirmed their worst fears.

Mr. Ford states in his letter that deceased

About 1877

Georgia Ann Hattie

J. V. Norton
about 1877

1911

G. B. N.

38. Henrietta Maria Schenck, VIII., daughter of Benjamin Baird (6) and Harriet (Sullivan) Schenck, was born at Plainville, N. Y., November 10, 1843, and March 20, 1864, married John Vedder Norton, son of Lyman and Ann Norton, and grandson of Aaron F. and Nancy Vedder. (See p. 83.) He was born November 7, 1840.

They had three children:— *Died*

107 I. Georgianna Belle, born at Plainville, N. Y., October 16, 1864. Address, 3719 W. 32nd. Ave., Denver, Colo.

108 II. Harriet Maria was born at Plainville, N. Y., June 20, 1866, and died at Memphis, N. Y., August 18, 1877.

109 III. Ann was born at Plainville, N. Y., January 13, 1869, and died at the same place, May 6, 1876.

John Vedder Norton died at Rio Janeiro, Brazil, February 11, 1879, and January 31, 1883, Henrietta (Schenck) Norton (38) married Daniel James Fitzgerald, son of John and Nancy Fitzgerald. He was born at Syracuse, N. Y., June 27, 1834, and died at Denver, Colo., December 26, 1904.

Henrietta (Schenck, Norton) Fitzgerald: Address, 3719 W. 32nd. Ave., Denver, Colo.

39. Burns Spaulding, VIII., son of Solomon B. and Eliza (Schenck) Spaulding (7), was born at Plainville, N. Y., March 25, 1833, and October 26, 1856, married Caroline A. Phelps, daughter of H. Nelson and Mary Phelps. (See p. 92.) She was born in Sullivan Township, Madison County, N. Y., October 18, 1835.

They had two children:—

110 I.   Inez Eudora, born November 22, 1857.   See p. 112.
111 II. Irving Burns was born at Rochester, N. Y., May 4, 1869, and died there October 14, 1869.

Burns Spaulding (39) died at Kankakee, Ill., April 24, 1893.   Caroline A. (Phelps) Spaulding died at Chicago, Ill., May 2, 1907.

40.   Mary C. Spaulding, VIII., daughter of Solomon B. and Eliza (Schenck) Spaulding (7), was born at Plainville, N. Y., October 30, 1837, and February 2, 1860, married Major Fitts Phelps, son of H. Nelson and Mary Phelps.   (See p. 91.)   He was born at Chittenango, Madison County, N. Y., March 15, 1834.

They had two children:—

112 I.   Louis Spaulding, born May 27, 1862.   See p. 113.
113 II. Homer Jay, born September 5, 1866.   See p. 113.

Mary (Spaulding) Phelps (40) died June 21, 1906. Major F. Phelps died at Fulton, N. Y., June 20, 1907.

41.   Annie Laura Spaulding, VIII., daughter of Solomon B. and Eliza (Schenck) Spaulding (7), was born at Plainville, N. Y., April 28, 1843, and December 17, 1863, married J. Edward Perkins, son of Erastus B. and Sarah Perkins.   He was born at Syracuse, N. Y., March 13, 1834.   They have no children.

Annie Laura (Spaulding) Perkins (41):   Address, Kirkville, N. Y.

42.   Dealia Spaulding, VIII., daughter of Solomon B. and Eliza (Schenck) Spaulding (7), was born at Plainville, N. Y., February 2, 1850, and October 15, 1874, married L. Austin Chapman, son of Austin and Adelia Chapman.   He was born at South Granby, Oswego County, N. Y., February 18, 1853.

They had three children:

114 I. Irwin B. was born at South Granby, N. Y., March 4, 1879, and died June 16, 1879.

115 II. Earl Burns, born June 12, 1880. See p. 114.

116 III. Hazel Eliza, born February 6, 1889. See p. 114.

Dealia (Spaulding) Chapman (42) died at Fulton, N. Y., June 28, 1890. L. Austin Chapman: Address, Fulton, N. Y.

44. James Rulef Fenner, VIII., son of Frederick W. and Eleanor (Schenck) Fenner (9) was born in Lysander Township, Onondaga County, N. Y., August 12, 1836, and March 27, 1859, married Ellen A. Savage, daughter of Seth and Emily Savage. She was born at Cazenovia, N. Y., July 8, 1839.

They had two children:—

117 I. James Emory, born June 4, 1862. See p. 115.

118 II. Florence Ellen, born February 18, 1877. See p. 115.

Ellen A. (Savage) Fenner died at Delphi, N. Y., February 13, 1897, and January 19, 1898, James Rulef (44) married Mrs. Addie E. Barber, born at Fabius, Onondaga County, N. Y., November 28, 1843.

Addie E. (Barber) Fenner died May 3, 1899, and February 20, 1900, James Rulef (44) married Mrs. Leida Jones, born at Burwell, Ontario, January 27, 1856. James Rulef Fenner (44) died March 1, 1909, at Delphi Falls, N. Y.

46. Sarah Ellen Fenner, VIII., daughter of Frederick W. and Eleanor (Schenck) Fenner (9) was born in Lysander Township, Onondaga County, N. Y., September 3, 1841, and September 8, 1863, married Sylvester

A. Vedder, son of Francis P. and Wilmina (Terhune) Vedder, cousin of John Vedder Norton (see p. 91) and nephew of James S. Vedder. (See p. 83.) Sylvester A. Vedder was born at Plainville, N. Y., September 19, 1834.

They had seven children:

   119 I. Frederick Fenner, born October 26, 1866. See p. 116.

   120 II. Nicholas was born October 19, 1868, and died October 20, 1868.

   121 III. Wilmina Wycoff, born September 17, 1872. See p. 116.

   122 IV. Ross Sylvester, born November 8, 1874. See p. 116.

   123 V. George Barry was born at Carrollton, Ill., January 25, 1878, and died there August 26, 1898.

   124 VI. Neil Davis, born October 29, 1880. See p. 117.

   125 VII. Clyde Byron was born at Carrollton, July 25, 1883, and died there January 5, 1885.

Sylvester A. Vedder died at Carrollton, Ill., March 19, 1907. Sarah Ellen (Fenner) Vedder (46): Address, Carrollton, Ill.

47. Frederick William Fenner, VIII., son of Frederick W. and Eleanor (Schenck) Fenner (9), was born in Lysander, Onondaga County, N. Y., June 11, 1847, and March 17, 1866, married Eliza Day, daughter of Hezekiah and Eliza Ann Day, and a sister of Adaline (Day) Schenck. (See p. 83.) She was born in Lysander Township, September 19, 1847.

They had two children:—

   126 I. Charles Day, born August 18, 1867. See p. 117.

   127 II. Frederick William, born November 10, 1869. See p. 117.

Frederick William Fenner (47): Address, Baldwinsville, N. Y.

49. Byron Russell Fenner, VIII., son of Russell B.
and Hannah (Schenck) Fenner (10), was born at Lysander, Onondaga County, N. Y., March 4, 1839, and January 1, 1861, married Caroline V. Nash, daughter of
Major D. and Phoebe Nash. She was born in Gunplain, Allegan County, Mich., June 30, 1841.

They had four children:—

128 I. Byron Nash, born in Gunplain, Mich., July 4,
1862. Address, Cressey, Mich.

129 II. Jennie, born August 15, 1864. See p. 118.

130 III. William Perry was born in Gunplain, Mich., October 17, 1866, and died there May 8, 1869.

131 IV. Nina Vanderveer, born at Prairieville, Barry County, Mich., April 21, 1879.

Byron Russell Fenner (49) died July 18, 1904. Caroline (Nash) Fenner: Address, Cressey, Mich.

50. Eliza Eleanor Fenner, VIII., daughter of Russell
B. and Hannah V. (Schenck) Fenner (10), was born in
Lysander, Onondaga County, N. Y., April 1, 1842, and
July 3, 1859, married Henry Robley Scott, son of Ira
and Mary B. Scott. He was born at LeRoy, Genesee
County, N. Y., August 17, 1836.

They had eight children:—

132 I. Mary Eleanor was born in Gunplain, Allegan
County, Mich., May 21, 1860, and died January 1,
1864.

133 II. William Henry, born January 28, 1863. See p. 118.

134 III. Kittie Belle, born December 21, 1864. See p. 119.

135 IV. Charles Seneca, born January 12, 1869. See p. 119.

136 V. Herbert Russell, born September 27, 1871. See p.
119.

137 VI. Franklin James, born September 30, 1873. See p. 120.

138 VII. Bertha May, born August 4, 1875. See p. 120.

139 VIII. Caroline Eleanor, born August 2, 1877. See p. 120.

Henry Robley Scott died June 8, 1905. Eliza Eleanor (Fenner) Scott (50): Address, Plainwell, Mich.

51. William Perry Fenner, VIII., son of Russell B. and Hannah V. (Schenck) Fenner (10), was born at Martin, Allegan County, Mich., December 22, 1844, and December 22, 1869, married Mina L. Sornbury, daughter of Horace and Elizabeth (Hicks) Sornbury. She was born at Martin, Mich., December 31, 1844.

They had six children:—

140 I. Ernest William, born September 24, 1870. See p. 121.

141 II. Nellie May, born September 1, 1872. See p. 121.

142 III. James Bruce, born September 28, 1874. See p. 121.

143 IV. Hannah Jane, born in Gunplain Township, Allegan County, Mich., January 3, 1877.

144 V. Pearl Eliza, born in Gunplain Township, Allegan County, Mich., August 10, 1880.

145 VI. Orlie Perry, born December 20, 1884. See p. 122.

Mina (Sornbury) Fenner died at Martin, Mich., February 11, 1908. William Perry Fenner (51): Address, Martin, Mich.

52. Rulef James Fenner, VIII., son of Russell B. and Hannah V. (Schenck) Fenner (10) was born at Martin, Allegan County, Mich., September 17, 1850, and April 12, 1876, married Mary Elizabeth Case, daughter of Stephen and Sarah Case. She was born at Lynden, Cattaraugus County, N. Y., October 5, 1851.

Children:—

146 I. Elton Perry, born in Watson, Allegan County, Mich., July 26, 1881. Address, Martin, Mich.

Rulef James Fenner (52): Address, Martin, Mich.

53. Franklin Monroe Fenner, VIII., son of Russell B. and Hannah V. (Schenck) Fenner (10), was born in Martin, Allegan County, Mich., October 11, 1854, and October 11, 1877, married Hannah Ida Honeysett, daughter of James and Hannah Honeysett. She was born in Gunplain, Mich., July 24, 1858.

Children:—

147 I. Edith May. born October 23, 1878. See p. 122.
148 II. Ida Myrtle, born July 17, 1880. See p. 123.
149 III. Starr Franklin, born February 24, 1886. See p. 123.
150 IV. Clay Earl, born in Gunplain, Mich., March 15, 1889. Address, Plainwell, Mich.
151 V. Wave Iola, born in Gunplain, 'Mich., May 25, 1895. Address, Plainwell, Mich.

Franklin Monroe Fenner (53): Address, R. F. D. No. 2, Plainwell, Mich.

54. Hulbert Luke Schenck, VIII., son of William Baird (11) and Catherine (Vanderveer) Schenck, was born in Savannah, Wayne County, N. Y., December 6, 1843, and January 12, 1865, married Betsey Fenner, daughter of John and Zilpha (Washburn) Fenner and niece of Frederick W. and Russell B. Fenner (see p. 74). She was born in Lysander, Onondaga County, N. Y., March 12, 1844.

They had two children:—

152 I. Nellie Maria, born September 11, 1867. See p. 123.
153 II. William Vanderveer, born January 22, 1875. See p. 124.

Hulbert Luke Schenck (54) died in Lysander, N. Y., March 14, 1879. Betsey (Fenner) Schenck: Address, R. F. D., Memphis, N. Y.

55. Irwin Vanderveer Schenck, VIII., son of William Baird (11) and Catherine M. (Vanderveer) Schenck, was born in Lysander Township, Onondaga County, N. Y., November 2, 1846, and December 9, 1868, married Ann Hubble Tator (64), daughter of James M. and Jane Ann (Wilson) Tator (17). She was born September 7, 1849, and died August 17, 1894. Irwin Vanderveer Schenck (55) died October 5, 1902. They left no children.

56. James Shuler Schenck, VIII., son of William Baird (11) and Catherine M. (Vanderveer) Schenck, was born in the Township of Lysander, Onondaga County, N. Y., August 19, 1851, and December 17, 1873, married Ella Lucretia Wormuth, daughter of Solomon and Charlotte Wormuth. She was born in Lysander, N. Y., July 31, 1854.

Children:—

154 I. Lester Hulbert, born August 4, 1880. See p. 124.

James Shuler Schenck (56): Address, R. F. D., Memphis, N. Y.

58. Lelia Maria Schenck, VIII., daughter of James L. (12) and Nancy Maria (Sullivan) Schenck, was born at Plainville, N. Y., November 8, 1856, and June 26, 1883, married T. Edgar Pomeroy, son of Dr. Theodore C. and Theresa M. (Elder) Pomeroy. He was born at Onondaga Valley, N. Y., December 25, 1846.

DIED.

POMEROY—Wednesday morning, Oct. 19 1892, Lelia M. Schenck, wife of T. Edgar Pomeroy, aged 35 years. Funeral at the family residence, 208 Van Buren street, Syracuse. Friends are invited. Burial private.

DEATHS.

POMEROY—In the town of Salina, Dec. 27, 1905, Edgar Pomeroy, aged 59 years. Private funeral services from his late home, 125 Harold-st., Friday, Dec. 29. Burial at Oakwood.

They had three children:—

155 I.   Clara Lelia was born at Syracuse, N. Y., September 24, 1886, and died there January 10, 1887.

156 II. Edgar Schenck, born at Syracuse, N. Y., July 17, 1889. Address, 104 Lynhurst St., Syracuse, N. Y.

157 III. Harold Eltweed was born at Syracuse, N. Y., February 6, 1891, and died there October 15, 1891.

Lelia Maria (Schenck) Pomeroy (58) died at Syracuse, N. Y., October 19, 1892, and June 23, 1903, T. Edgar Pomeroy married Melissa Almira Weller. He died at Syracuse, December 27, 1905.

60.   Effie Isadore Schenck, VIII., daughter of Rulef (13) and Emerancy Jane (Emerick) Schenck, was born at the Homestead, Lysander Township, Onondaga County, N. Y., February 12, 1854, and May 4, 1871, married George William Simmons, son of Peter and Elizabeth Simmons. He was born in New Scotland, Albany County, N. Y., July 28, 1851.

Children:—

158 1. Elva, born August 31, 1871. See page 125.

159 II. Raymond Percy was born in Cato Township, Cayuga County, N. Y., September 8, 1874, and died there March 20, 1889.

Effie Isadore (Schenck) Simmons (60): Address, R. F. D., Cato, N. Y.

61.   William Baird Schenck, VIII., son of Rulef (13) and Emerancy Jane (Emerick) Schenck, was born at the Homestead, Lysander Township, Onondaga County, N. Y., July 21, 1859, and July 13, 1879, married Florence Loretta Osborn, daughter of David and Margaret Ann Osborn. She was born in Lysander, N. Y., July 8, 1863.

Children:—

 160 I. Florence Loretta, born August 3, 1880. See p. 125.
 161 II. Rulef David, born January 21, 1885. See p. 125.

William Baird Schenck (61): Address, 13 W. Main St., Cortland, N. Y.

NINTH GENERATION IN AMERICA.

 62. Mervin James Wilson, IX., son of Austin Wycoff (14) and Mary Ann (Verity) Wilson, was born at Plainville, Onondaga County, N. Y., May 5, 1850, and June 27, 1871, married Minnie Ann Locke, daughter of John V. N. and Ann Locke. She was born February 24, 1853, and died July 15, 1872. They had no children. Mervin James married March 23, 1880, Cornelia Harrington, daughter of Thomas and Catherine Harrington. She was born at Jordan, N. Y., May 12, 1861.

Children:—

 162 I. Ada Mary, born January 1, 1881. See p. 126.

Mervin James Wilson (62): Address, Meridian, N. Y.

 63. Orinda More Wilson, IX., daughter of Dennis Kennedy (16) and Lydia Amanda (Tator) Wilson, was born in Lysander Township, Onondaga County, N. Y., November 23, 1850, and February 19, 1867, married Delancy Duyane Stone, son of Alpheus and Lucy Ann Stone. He was born January 8, 1846.

They had three children:—

 163 I. Willard Dennis, born June 7, 1870. See p. 126.
 164 II. Rosa Anna, born October 5, 1879. See p. 127.
 165 III. Jennie Lucy was born in Lysander Township, Onondaga County, N. Y., July 2, 1884, and died at Baldwinsville, N. Y., December 9, 1887.

Delancy Duyane Stone died August 1, 1898. Orinda More (Wilson) Stone (63) : Address, Auburn, N. Y.

64. Ann Hubble Tator, IX., daughter of James M. and Jane Ann (Wilson) Tator (17), was born September 7, 1849, and December 9, 1868, married Irwin Vanderveer Schenck (55). (See p. 98.)

67. John Schenck Voorhees, IX., son of James L. and Parna Eleanora (Schenck) Voorhees (24), was born in Lysander Township, Onondaga County, N. Y., August 11, 1856, and June 7, 1905, married Anna Cornelia Moerschler, daughter of John and Caroline (Nulty) Moerschler. She was born at Syracuse, N. Y., July 2, 1877.

Children :—
    166 I. Son, born May 31, 1906. Died in infancy.
    167 II. Henry Austin, born May 27, 1907.
John Schenck Voorhees (67) : Address, Baldwinsville, N. Y.

69. Henry Peter Voorhees, IX., son of James L. and Parna Eleanora (Schenck) Voorhees (24), was born December 1, 1861, and March 21, 1886, married Lillian B. Wells, daughter of Dr. James F. and Eveline (Bailey) Wells. She was born February 10, 1863. They had no children.

Henry Peter Voorhees (69) died at Baldwinsville, N. Y., February 9, 1889. Lillian (Wells) Voorhees married, June 6, 1901, Ralph Sheldon.

70. Inez Ann Vedder, IX., daughter of James S. and Harriet Livona (Schenck) Vedder (25), was born at Carrollton, Greene County, Ill., July 25, 1854, and Sep-

tember 3, 1873, married Joseph Garret Lowe, son of Ausborn E. and Sarah J. Lowe. He was born at Rushville, Ind., December 31, 1846.

They had eight children:—

168 I. Harriet Belle, born June 23, 1874. See p. 127.
169 II. Russell Gordon, born November 12, 1877. See p. 127.
170 III. Clara Leslie, born May 31, 1880. See p. 128.
171 IV. Joseph Garret, born October 22, 1883. Address, First National Bank, Wellston, Mo.
172 V. Richard Vedder was born at Washington, Kan., September 12, 1886, and died at El Reno, Okla., June 4, 1902.
173 VI. Bessie Inez, born at Washington, Kan., March 30, 1891.
174 VII. Mildred Adeline, born at Washington, Kan., January 8, 1894.
175 VIII. Ruth Marjorie, born at Washington, Kan., September 12, 1895.

Joseph Garret Lowe died at Piedmont, Okla., September 11, 1908. Inez Ann (Vedder) Lowe (70): Address, El Reno, Okla.

71. Harriet Elnora Vedder, IX., daughter of James S. and Harriet Livona (Schenck) Vedder (25), was born at Carrollton, Greene County, Ill., December 1, 1856, and September 3, 1874, married Alfred Mortimer Hallowell, son of Jesse R. and Penelope A. Hallowell. He was born at Middletown, O., February 20, 1847.

They had five children:—

176 I. Maud May, born April 13, 1876. See p. 128.
177 II. Roscoe Vedder was born at Washington, Kan., December 17, 1877, and died there January 7, 1880.
178 III. Henry Raymond was born at Washington, Kan., April 2, 1881, and died there July 24, 1882.

179 IV.   Edith Leona was born at Washington, Kan., November 20, 1882. Address, Ventura, Cal.

180 V.   Lyman Earl was born at Washington, Kan., April 21, 1885. Address, Winnipeg, Manitoba.

Harriet Elnora (Vedder) Hallowell (71) married, January 1, 1903, Charles Gordon Burtnett, born December 13, 1852. Harriet Elnora (Vedder-Hollowell) Burtnett (71): Address, Ventura, Cal.

72.   Lyman Norton Vedder, IX., son of James S. and Harriet Livona (Schenck) Vedder (25), was born at Carrollton, Greene County, Ill., November 27, 1858, and July 13, 1896, married Ernestine Adele Eddy, daughter of Lucien Crane and Amy (Kennedy) Eddy. She was born at Pella, Iowa, November 23, 1870.

Lyman Norton Vedder (72): Address, Anadarko, Okla.

74.   Floyd Sullivan Schenck, IX., son of John Sullivan (27) and Adaline (Day) Schenck, was born at Plainville, Onondaga County, N. Y., September 21, 1874, and November 3, 1895, married Olive Mastin, daughter of Allen Snyder and Lillian (Lindsay) Mastin. She was born at Plainville, N. Y., August 19, 1877.

They had one child:—

181 I.   Mildred Louise, born at Plainville, N. Y., January 19, 1897.

Floyd Sullivan Schenck (74) died at Plainville, N. Y., August 29, 1898, and January 14, 1902, Olive (Mastin) Schenck married Sardis A. Dunham, son of Joseph and Mary A. (Greenfield) Dunham. He was born at Baldwinsville, N. Y., July 10, 1876.

Olive (Mastin-Schenck) Dunham: Address, 545 Cedar St., Syracuse, N. Y.

75. Charles Fred Smith, IX., son of Charles and Perlina Adele (Schenck) Smith (29), was born at Washington, Kan., December 12, 1874, and June 29, 1908,
married Elizabeth Abigail Townsend, daughter of Joseph
R. and Mary J. (Baker) Townsend. She was born at
Cottage Home, Ill., March 13, 1878.
Children:—

182 I. Elizabeth Gertrude, born at Oklahoma City, Okla.,
August 28, 1909.

Charles Fred Smith (75): Attorney-at-Law, Address,
335 Lee Building, Oklahoma City, Okla.

76. Nellie Leslie Smith, IX., daughter of Charles and
Perlina Adele (Schenck) Smith (29), was born at Wash-
ington, Kan., January 27, 1876, and February 20, 1894,
married Eddie A. Vincent, son of Reuben and Alice
(Larabee) Vincent. He was born at Crown Point, Ind.,
February 17, 1871.
They had one child:—

183 I. Adele Pauline was born at Washington, Kan.,
October 11, 1897.

Eddie A. Vincent died at Albuquerque, N. M., September 18, 1903, and May 1, 1908, Nellie Leslie (Smith)
Vincent (76) married John A. Kinch, son of Samuel R.
and Abigail Ann (Groff) Kinch. He was born at Columbia, Pa., September 23, 1876.
Children:—

184 I. Infant, unnamed, born and died at Oklahoma City,
January 31, 1909.
185 II. Kathryn Augusta, born at Oklahoma City, Okla.,
April 19, 1910.

Nellie Leslie (Smith-Vincent) Kinch (76): Address,
432 West 6th St., Oklahoma City, Okla.

77. Joseph Lowe Smith, IX., son of Charles and Perlina Adele (Schenck) Smith (29), was born at Washington, Kan., November 23, 1877, and March 20, 1904, married Florence Elser, daughter of John Joshua and Anna (Burke) Elser. She was born at Harlan, Iowa, February 25, 1881.

Children:—

    186 I. Charles Elser, born at Washington, Kan., April 23, 1907.

Joseph Lowe Smith (77) received the degree of D. D. S. at the Dental Department of Denver University, in 1906. Address: First National Bank Building, Washington, Kan.

78. Harry James Smith, IX., son of Charles and Perlina Adele (Schenck) Smith (29), was born at Washington, Kan., September 30, 1883, and May 24, 1905, married Loula Anna Hill, daughter of Harvey Cooney and Elizabeth (Finley) Hill. She was born at Washington, Kan., October 13, 1882.

Harry James Smith (78): Address, 340 Board of Trade, Kansas City, Mo.

79. Harriet Marie Smith, IX., daughter of Charles and Perlina Adele (Schenck) Smith (29), was born at Washington, Kan., May 16, 1885, and May 31, 1910, married Axel Walfred Erickson, son of Erik Axel and Hedda Louise (Jonson) Erickson. He was born at Trosa, Sweden, August 2, 1882.

Harriet Marie (Smith) Erickson (79): Address, Lindsborg, Kan.

81. Lisle John Schenck, IX., son of Benjamin Freeman (30) and Eliza (Chittenden) Schenck, was born at Plainville, Onondaga County, N. Y., June 10, 1879, and October 27, 1910, married Lulu May Wilson, daughter of George W. and Margaret (Otis) Wilson. She was born at Baldwinsville, N. Y., May 10, 1883.

Lisle John Schenck (81): Address, Baldwinsville, N. Y.

82. Elsie May Schenck, IX., daughter of Benjamin Freeman (30) and Ella Eliza (Chittenden) Schenck, was born at Plainville, N. Y., May 7, 1881, and June 22, 1904, married Frederick L. Huntington, son of Henry L. and Mary (Fisher) Huntington. He was born at Lysander, N. Y., September 3, 1883.

Children:—

    187 I. Lisle Schenck, born at Plainville, N. Y., May 21, 1906.

Elsie May (Schenck) Huntington (82): Address, Plainville, N. Y.

83. Frank Leslie Bratt, IX., son of John (32) and Matilda Wilson Bratt, was born in Lysander Township, Onondaga County, N. Y., November 1, 1857, and September 8, 1878, married Jennie Stickle, daughter of Elizabeth and Jacob Stickle. She was born at Peru, N. Y., July 14, 1860. They had no children.

Jennie (Stickle) Bratt died February 26, 1885, and August 6, 1886, Frank Leslie Bratt (83) married Ella Babcock, daughter of David and Margaret Babcock. She was born at Belleville, Ont., December 25, 1866. They had no children.

Ella (Babcock) Bratt died January 14, 1903, and September 4, 1904, Frank Leslie Bratt (83) married Lillian Miller, daughter of Albert and Mary Miller. She was born at West Leyden, N. Y., February 1, 1872.

Frank Leslie Bratt (83) died at Munnsville, N. Y., December 27, 1910.

84. Charles Willis Bratt, IX., son of John (32) and Matilda (Wilson) Bratt, was born at Togg, Lysander Township, Onondaga County, N. Y., May 31, 1859, and April 5, 1883, married Nettie Matilda Horton, daughter of Edward and Mary Horton. She was born at Hortontown, Lysander Township, N. Y., June 3, 1859.

They had two children:—

188 I. Jessie Belle, born May 2, 1884. See p. 128.
189 II. Lela Jane, born November 25, 1889, and died August 7, 1890.

Nettie Matilda (Horton) Bratt died December 25, 1894, and March, 1904, Charles Willis Bratt (84) married Hattie Osborn Humphrey, born June 6, 1859. Charles Willis Bratt (84): Address, 79 Scribner St., Grand Rapids, Mich.

85. Ella May Bratt, IX., daughter of John (32) and Matilda (Wilson) Bratt, was born at Togg, Lysander Township, Onandaga County, N. Y., September 21, 1862, and December 9, 1879, married Garret L. Vanderveer, son of Henry and Agnes Mary Vanderveer and grandson of Garret Vanderveer. (See p. 79.) He was born near Plainville, N. Y., September 27, 1858.

They had three children:—

190 I. Hattie May, born October 5, 1881. See p. 129.
191 II. Henry was born at Plainville, N. Y., May 15, 1884, and died June 7, 1892.

192 III. John Pomyea, born at Plainville, N. Y., January 17,
    1886. Address, Lysander, N. Y.

Ella May (Bratt) Vanderveer (85) died at Plainville,
N. Y., December 11, 1888. Garret L. Vanderveer died
at Meridian, N. Y., July 3, 1907.

86.   Anna Isabell Bratt, IX., daughter of John (32)
and Matilda (Wilson) Bratt, was born at Plainville, N.
Y., August 9, 1864, and January 17, 1885, married John
Wesley Albright, son of Jacob and Eliza (Reed) Albright.
He was born at New Scotland, Albany County, N. Y.,
May 8, 1859.

Children:—

193 I. Charles Wesley, born at Hurstville, Albany Coun-
    ty, N. Y., May 14, 1889.
194 II. Howard Baxter, born at Hurstville, N. Y., July 23,
    1895.
195 III. Wesley Alfred, born at Hurstville, N. Y., April 9,
    1897.
196 IV. Henry Cary, born at New Scotland, Albany County,
    N. Y., August 23, 1903.

Anna Isabell (Bratt) Albright (86): Address, R. F.
D., Voorheesville, N. Y.

87.   Alice Merriman Bratt, IX., daughter of John
(32) and Matilda (Wilson) Bratt, was born at Plainville, Onondaga County, N. Y., September 11, 1866, and
January 14, 1885, married Edward Alexander Jackson,
son of Richard and Mary (Clark) Jackson. He was born
at Scroepples, N. Y., December 30, 1860.

Children:—

197 I. Eyola Bratt, born at Plainville, N. Y., October
    21, 1888.
198 II. Reba Mary was born at Baldwinsville, N. Y., June
    4, 1894, and died June 21, 1898.

Alice Merriman (Bratt) Jackson (87) : Address, Bald winsville, N. Y.

88. Ernest Wilson Bratt, IX., son of John (32) and Matilda (Wilson) Bratt, was born at Plainville, Onondaga County, N. Y., December 26, 1869, and February 11, 1891. married Julia Stevens, daughter of John and Eleanor Stevens. She was born at Buffalo, N. Y., November 20, 1869.

Children:—

    199 I. Florence May, born at Grand Rapids, Mich., June 7, 1892.

    200 II. Alice Viola, born at Grand Rapids, Mich., March 13, 1896.

Ernest Wilson Bratt (88) : Address, Edgerton, Mich.

89. Sarah Elsie Bratt, IX., daughter of John (32) and Matilda (Wilson) Bratt, was born at Plainville, Onondaga County, N. Y., November 12, 1872, and January 20, 1897, married Franklin Mills Adsit, son of Francis and Mary (Mills) Adsit. He was born at Little Utica, Onondaga County, N. Y., March 21, 1871.

Children:—

    201 I. Elon Bratt, born at Little Utica, N. Y., January 15, 1899.

Sarah Elsie (Bratt) Adsit (89) : Address, Baldwinsville, N. Y.

90. Ella Lillian Hubbard, IX., daughter of Chauncey and Elsie (Bratt) Hubbard (33), was born at Plainville, Onondaga County, N. Y., December 31, 1854, and March 26, 1878, married Miles Clarence Carncross, son of John and Mary Ann (Elsworth) Carncross. He was born at Meridian, Cayuga County, N. Y., October 22, 1855.

Children:—

202 I.   Avis May, born January 31, 1884. See p. 129.
203 II. Frank Hubbard, born at Plainville, N. Y., March 23, 1893.

Ella Lillian (Hubbard) Carncross (90): Address, Plainville, N. Y.

97.   Herbert Eugene Bratt, IX., son of Peter Schenck (35) and Marta Nettie (Carpenter) Bratt, was born in the Township of Lysander, Onondaga County, February 13, 1870, and January 26, 1890, married Frances E. Hammond, daughter of George and Hettie Hammond. She was born at Lysander, N. Y., May 12, 1868.

Children:—

204 I.   Earl, born in Lysander Township, Onondaga County, N. Y., February 18, 1891.
205 II.   Glenn, born in Lysander Township, N. Y., August 18, 1892.
206 III. Frances was born in Lysander Township, N. Y., March 12, 1895, and died March 30, 1895.
207 IV. Mabel was born in Lysander Township, N. Y., May 12, 1896.
208 V.   Ethel, born in Lysander Township, N. Y., October 12, 1898.
209 VI. Edith, born in Lysander Township, N. Y., January 7, 1901.

Herbert Eugene Bratt (97): Address, R. F. D., Memphis, N. Y.

98.   LeRoy Bratt, IX., son of Peter Schenck (35) and Marta Nettie (Carpenter) Bratt, was born in Lysander Township, Onondaga County, N. Y., July 23, 1872, and October 24, 1890, married Grace Hall, daughter of Robert and Frances (Carson) Hall. She was born at Mauston, Wis., September 8, 1870.

Children:—

   210 I. Florence Louise, born at Syracuse, N. Y., August 30, 1902.

   211 II. Gertrude Ruth, born at Syracuse, N. Y., September 16, 1907.

LeRoy Bratt (98): Address, 257 Fitch St., Syracuse, N. Y.

99. Arthur Bratt, IX., son of Peter Schenck (35) and Marta Nettie (Carpenter) Bratt, was born in Lysander Township, Onondaga County, N. Y., February 28, 1874, and April 7, 1897, married Grace Edna Gibbs, daughter of William and Augusta Gibbs. She was born at Jordan, N. Y., April 15, 1872.

Arthur Bratt (99): Address, Jordan, N. Y.

100. William Peter Bratt, IX., son of Peter Schenck (35) and Marta Nettie (Carpenter) Bratt, was born in Lysander Township, Onondaga County, N. Y., December 17, 1882, and January 4, 1905, married Maude Bowman, daughter of Willis and Alice (Farley) Bowman. She was born at Memphis, N. Y., July 10, 1878.

William Peter Bratt (100): Address, Memphis, N. Y.

101. Harry Bratt, IX., son of Peter Schenck (35) and Marta Nettie (Carpenter) Bratt, was born in the Township of Lysander, Onondaga County, N. Y., August 26, 1884, and June 24, 1909, married Iona Leona Doane, daughter of Adelbert and Anna (Van Slyck) Doane. She was born at Syracuse, N. Y., November 22, 1883.

Harry Bratt (101): Address, 402 Arthur St., Syracuse, N. Y.

102. Raymond Bratt, IX., son of Peter Schenck (35) and Marta Nettie (Carpenter) Bratt was born in Lysander Township, Onondaga County, N. Y., August 24, 1888, and January 1, 1910, married Martha Jessie Rogers, daughter of Frank Adelbert and Elizabeth (Bittel) Rogers. She was born in Lysander Township, April 1, 1888.

Raymond Bratt (102): Address, Baldwinsville, N. Y.

105. Benjamin Robinson Schenck, IX., son of Adrian Adelbert (37) ,and Harriet Parthenia (Robinson) Schenck, was born at Syracuse, N. Y., August 19, 1872, and August 17, 1904, married Jessie Jane McCallum, daughter of Peter and Agnes (McIndoe) McCallum. She was born at St. Catharines, Ont., August 10, 1872.

Children:—

> 212 I. Leila Marion, born at Detroit, Mich., September 30, 1905.
> 213 II. John Tyler, born at Detroit, Mich., September 18, 1907.

Benjamin Robinson Schenck (105) received the degree of A. B. from Williams College in 1894, and the degree of M. D. from Johns Hopkins University in 1898. Address: 32 Adams Ave., W., Detroit, Mich.

110. Inez Eudora Spaulding, IX., daughter of Burns (39) and Caroline A. (Phelps) Spaulding, was born at Plainville, Onondaga County, N. Y., November 22, 1857, and April 10, 1878, married Charles Watson Kyle, son of Alexander and Caroline A. Kyle. He was born in New York City, May 13, 1844.

They had one child:—

> 214 I. Caroline Inez, born at Detroit, Mich., August 22, 1879.

Inez Eudora (Spaulding) Kyle (110), married May 24, 1894, Almeron Ward Dunsmore, son of Phineas H. and Lucy Juliette (Peters) Dunsmore. He was born at Fowlersville, N. Y., August 14, 1854.

Inez Eudora (Spaulding) Dunsmore (110): Address, 7300 Princeton Ave., Chicago, Ill.

112. Louis Spaulding Phelps, IX., son of Major Fitts and Mary (Spaulding) Phelps (40), was born at Granby, Oswego County, N. Y., May 27, 1862, and September 16, 1885, married Carrie M. Barnard, daughter of Selah Smith and Melissa (Parker) Barnard. She was born at Volney, N. Y., September 16, 1865.

They had three children:—

215 I. Harry Barrett, born August 9, 1886. See p. 130.
216 II. Homer Spaulding, born April 11, 1888. See p. 130.
217 III. Lena Marion, born at Fulton, N. Y., March 2, 1896.

Louis Spaulding Phelps (112) died at Banks, Oregon, June 17, 1908. Carrie M. (Barnard) Phelps: Address, Fulton, N. Y.

113. Homer Jay Phelps, IX., son of Major Fitts and Mary (Spaulding) Phelps (40), was born in Granby Township, Oswego County, N. Y., September 5, 1866, and July 3, 1890, married Sarah Agnes Ostrander, daughter of William Henry and Sarah Ellen (Goodman) Ostrander. She was born at Mottville, Onondaga County, N. Y., May 11, 1866.

Children:—

218 I. Eliza Eleanor, born at South Granby, N. Y., May 20, 1891.
219 II. Harold Major, born at Fulton, N. Y., March 23, 1893.

220 III. Anna Laura, born at South Granby, N. Y., November 9, 1894.

221 IV. Mildred Bessie, born at Fulton, N. Y., January 17, 1896.

222 V. Gertrude, born at Fulton, N. Y., February 7, 1898.

223 VI. Raymond Lee, born at Fulton, N. Y., April 4, 1900.

224 VII. Alfred was born at Fulton, N. Y., December 8, 1902, and died there May 23, 1903.

225 VIII. Ruth Marjorie, born at Fulton, N. Y., June 20, 1904.

Homer Jay Phelps (113): Address, Fulton, N. Y.

115. Earl Burns Chapman, IX., son of L. Austin and Dealia (Spaulding) Chapman (42), was born at South Granby, Oswego County, N. Y., June 12, 1880, and October 30, 1903, married Minnie Mae Schall, daughter of Ephraim and Ellen (McKinney) Schall. She was born at Beach Bottom, Elk County, Pa., April 12, 1881.

Children:—

226 I. Minnie Geraldine, born at Burton, O., June 14, 1909.

Earl Burns Chapman (115): Address, American Express Company, Cleveland, O.

116. Hazel Eliza Chapman, IX., daughter of L. Austin and Dealia (Spaulding) Chapman (42), was born at South Granby, Oswego County, N. Y., February 6, 1889, and July 28, 1906, married Harry Albertus Ketchum, son of James Robert and Isadora (Ceathoat) Ketchum. He was born at Alger, Mich., December 26, 1886.

Children:—

227 I. Robert Burns, born at Fulton, N. Y., February 17, 1908.

Hazel Eliza (Chapman) Ketchum (116): Address, Fulton, N. Y.

117. James Emory Fenner, IX., son of James Rulef (44) and Ellen A. (Savage) Fenner, was born at Cazenovia, N. Y., June 4, 1862, and August 9, 1883, married Lou A. Pinckney, daughter of Alpheus and Julia Pinckney. She was born at Onondaga Valley, N. Y., March 12, 1864.

Children:—

228 I. Frederick Munroe, born at Onondaga Valley, N. Y., November 3, 1883, and now in the United States Marine Service. Enlisted September 17, 1906.

229 II. Harry Rulef, born at Delphi Falls, Onondaga County, N. Y., September 23, 1886.

230 III. Frank Clifton was born at Delphi Falls, N. Y., August 9, 1889, and died there September 7, 1890.

231 IV. Raymond Erasmus, born at Delphi Falls, N. Y., August 28, 1903.

James Emeroy Fenner (117): Address, Delphi Falls, N. Y.

118. Florence Ellen Fenner, IX., daughter of James Rulef (44) and Ellen A. (Savage) Fenner, was born at Delphi, Onondaga County, N. Y., February 18, 1877, and August 27, 1895, married Frederick Thomas Galloway, son of Henry and Harriet E. (Hitchcock) Galloway. He was born in Delphi, N. Y., September 6, 1871.

Children:—

232 I. Wilbur Fenner, born at Delphi, N. Y., March 29, 1896.

Florence Ellen (Fenner) Galloway (118): Address, 722 Cannon St., Syracuse, N. Y.

119. Frederick Fenner Vedder, IX., son of Sylvester A. and Sarah Ellen (Fenner) Vedder (46), was born at Carrollton, Ill., October 26, 1866, and February 25, 1892, married Cornelia Edna Vertrees, daughter of John and Frances (Fishback) Vertrees. She was born at Carrollton, Ill., April 14, 1868.

Children:—

    233 I. Virginia Vertrees, born at Carrollton, Ill., December 8, 1892.

    234 II. George Sidney, born at Carrollton, Ill., October 20, 1894.

Frederick Fenner Vedder (119) graduated from the Department of Pharmacy, University of Michigan, in 1886. Address, La Harpe, Ill.

121. Wilmina Wycoff Vedder, IX., daughter of Sylvester A. and Sarah Ellen (Fenner) Vedder (46), was born at Carrollton, Ill., September 17, 1872, and September 28, 1887, married John Cowan Wilson, son of Dr. Eberle and Lucy (Cannedy) Wilson. He was born at Fayette, Green County, Ill., August 21, 1869.

Children:—

    235 I. Eberle Irving, born at Carrollton, Ill., April 25, 1888.

Wilmina Wycoff (Vedder) Wilson (121) graduated at the Female Academy, Jacksonville, Ill., and at the Musical Conservatory of the same place. She later studied two years in the College of Music, Chicago. Address, 6938 Kimbark Ave., Chicago, Ill.

122. Ross Sylvester Vedder, IX., son of Sylvester A. and Sarah Ellen (Fenner) Vedder (46), was born at Carrollton, Ill., November 8, 1874, and August 22, 1900, married Kathleen Witherbee, daughter of Thomas F. and

Caroline (Pease) Witherbee. She was born at Port Henry, N. Y., June 9, 1880.

Ross Sylvester Vedder (122) graduated at the Chicago Dental College in 1897. Address, Nevada, Mo.

124. Neil Davis Vedder, IX., son of Sylvester A. and Sarah Ellen (Fenner) Vedder (46), was born at Carrollton, Ill., October 29, 1880, and June 6, 1906, married Edna Rumrill, daughter of Edward and Ella (Landiss) Rumrill. She was born at Carrollton, Ill., September 6, 1879.

Children:—

236 I. Herbert Edward, born at Carrollton, Ill., June 19, 1907.

Neil Davis Vedder (124) graduated from the Department of Dentistry, University of Michigan, 1901. Address, Carrollton, Ill.

126. Charles Day Fenner, IX., son of Frederick William (47) and Eliza (Day) Fenner, was born at Lysander, Onondaga County, N. Y., August 18, 1867, and June 4, 1890, married Mabel Keller, daughter of James Henry and Margaret (Martin) Keller. She was born at Lysander, N. Y., June 20, 1869.

Charles Day Fenner (126): Address, Baldwinsville, N. Y.

127. Frederick William Fenner, IX., son of Frederick William (47) and Eliza (Day) Fenner, was born at Lysander, Onondaga County, N. Y., November 10, 1869, and June 16, 1892, married Jessie Mead Kelly. She was born at Lysander, N. Y., May 11, 1872.

Children :—

237 I.   Halcyon Edith, born at Baldwinsville, N. Y., May
28, 1894.

Frederick William Fenner (127) : Address, 529 Tall-
man St., Syracuse, N. Y.

129. Jennie Fenner, IX., daughter of Byron Russell
(49) and Caroline V. (Nash) Fenner, was born in Gunplain Township, Allegan County, Mich., August 15,
1864, and February 12, 1890, married Manley Maurice
Chase, son of Hiram and Sarah (Holden) Chase.   He
was born at Prairieville, Mich., October 21, 1858.

Children :—

238. I.   Herbert Fenner was born at Prairieville, Mich.,
October 26, 1893, and died there January 15, 1894.

239 II.   Maurice Manley was born at Prairieville, Mich.,
March 28, 1896, and died there July 30, 1896.

240 III.   Elliott Leo was born at Prairieville, Mich., February 12, 1898, and died there April 1, 1899.

241 IV.   Cecile Caroline, born at Prairieville, Mich., March
15, 1899.

Jennie (Fenner) Chase (129) : Address, Prairieville,
Mich.

133. William Henry Scott, IX., son of Henry Robley
and Eliza Eleanor (Fenner) Scott (50), was born in
Gunplain Township, Allegan County, Mich., January
28, 1863, and July 2, 1882, married Allie Belle Phillips,
daughter of Albert and Harriet (Amsden) Phillips.   She
was born at Kendall Mills, Monroe County, N. Y,
April 22, 1864.

Children :—

242 I.   Maude Belle, born September 28, 1883.   See p. 130.

243 II.   Harry Agatha, born November 25, 1889.   See p.
131.

William Henry Scott (133): Address, 1607 E. Main St., Kalamazoo, Mich.

134. Kittie Belle Scott, IX., daughter of Henry Robley and Eliza Eleanor (Fenner) Scott (50), was born in Gunplain Township, Allegan County, Mich., December 21, 1864, and September 8, 1885, married John Franklin Eesley, son of Albert and Jennette (Goldie) Eesley. He was born at Hamilton, Ont., December 11, 1859.

Children:—

> 244 I. Iva Belle was born at Plainwell, Mich., June 8, 1887, and died there February 10, 1888.
> 245 II. Harold John, born in Plainwell, Mich., April 3, 1893.
> 246 III. Franklin R. B., was born in Plainwell, Mich., February 9, 1898, and died there October 21, 1898.

Kittie Belle (Scott) Eesley (134): Address, Plainwell, Mich.

135. Charles Seneca Scott, IX., son of Henry Robley and Eliza Eleanor (Fenner) Scott (50), was born at Plainwell, Mich., January 12, 1869, and April 5, 1893, married Belle A. Moulton, daughter of Irvin L. and Betsy E. (Wall) Moulton. She was born at Martin, Allegan County, Mich., October 20, 1872.

Children:—

> 247 I. Dorothea Moulton, born August 18, 1897.

Charles Seneca Scott (135): Address, Plainwell, Mich.

136. Herbert Russell Scott, IX., son of Henry Robley and Eliza Eleanor (Fenner) Scott (50), was born at Plainwell, Mich., September 27, 1871, and March 15, 1900, married Maud May Notter, daughter of John A.

and Jennie Lavinia (Burrows) Notter. She was born
at Flint, Mich., February 8, 1875.

Children:—

248 I. Herbert Russell, born June 20, 1903.
249 II. Donald Notter, born July 9, 1904.
250 III. Nathan Burrows, born October 23, 1908.
251 IV. Gerald Notter, born August 10, 1910.

Herbert Russell Scott (136): Address, 831 Clinton
Ave., Kalamazoo, Mich.

137. Franklin James Scott, IX., son of Henry Robley
and Eliza Eleanor (Fenner) Scott (50), was born at
Plainwell, Mich., September 30, 1873, and November
24, 1908, married Fannie Elizabeth Ransom, daughter
of John Noyes and Caroline (Hydorn) Ransom. She
was born at Alamo, Kalamazoo County, Mich., October
3, 1872.

Franklin James Scott (137): Address, Plainwell,
Mich.

138. Bertha May Scott, IX., daughter of Henry
Robley and Eliza Eleanor (Fenner) Scott (50), was born
at Plainwell, Mich., August 4, 1875, and November 11,
1904, married John Samuel McColl, son of John Thomas
and Isabella (McLean) McColl. He was born at Jackson, Mich., November 19, 1876.

Bertha May (Scott) McColl (138): Address, 415
Locust St., Kalamazoo, Mich.

139. Caroline Eleanor Scott, IX., daughter of Henry
Robley and Eliza Eleanor (Fenner) Scott (50), was
born at Plainwell, Mich., August 2, 1877, and July 8,
1908, married Ira R. Bullock, son of Ira and M. Josephine (Ensign) Bullock. He was born at Lynn, Mich.,
May 11, 1870.

Caroline Eleanor (Scott) Bullock (139): Address, Plainwell, Mich.

140. Ernest William Fenner, IX., son of William Perry (51) and Mina L. (Sornbury) Fenner, was born at Martin, Allegan County, Mich., September 24, 1870, and October 24, 1895, married Grace Nichols, daughter of Dr. George Byron and Eunice M. (Watkins) Nichols. She was born at Martin, Mich., November 9, 1870.

Children:—

 252 I. Horace Alfred, born at Martin, Mich., July 12, 1897.

 253 II. Helen Angeline, born at Martin, Mich., March 21, 1908.

 254 III. Byron Nichols, born at Martin, Mich., August 4, 1910.

Ernest William Fenner (140): Address, Martin, Mich.

141. Nellie May Fenner, IX., daughter of William Perry (51) and Mina L. (Sornbury) Fenner, was born in Gunplain Township, Allegan County, Mich., September 1, 1872, and January 30, 1896, married Frank A. Pratt, son of William and Emma (Buchanan) Pratt. He was born at Martin, Mich., January 25, 1872. Nellie (Fenner) Pratt died April 10, 1898, leaving no children.

142. James Bruce Fenner, IX., son of William Perry (51) and Mina L. (Sornbury) Fenner, was born in Gunplain Township, Allegan County, Mich., September 28, 1874, and April 14, 1897, married Wilma Belle Stayman, daughter of William D. and Mary J. (Swaney) Stayman. She was born at La Grange, Ind., December 7, 1875.

Children:—

255 I. Russell William, born at Martin, Mich., February 28, 1898.

256 II. Gertrude Helen, born at Martin, Mich., July 23, 1899.

James Bruce Fenner (142) died April 21, 1904. Wilma Belle (Stayman) Fenner: Address, Martin, Mich.

145. Orlie Perry Fenner, IX., son of William Perry (51) and Mina L. (Sornbury) Fenner, was born in Gunplain, Allegan County, Mich., December 20, 1884, and March 8, 1906, married Isabelle Ketchum, daughter of Fernando and Roxie (Presley) Ketchum. She was born at Martin, Mich., December 24, 1885.

Children:—

257 I. Gerald James, born in Martin, Allegan County, Mich., February 2, 1907.

258 II. Dorothy Isabelle, born in Martin, November 26, 1909.

Orlie Perry Fenner (145) now resides on the Homestead Farm in the Township of Martin, Allegan County, granted by the government to his grandfather Sornbury, about 1840. Address: Martin, Mich.

147. Edith May Fenner, IX., daughter of Franklin Monroe (53) and Hannah Ida (Honeysett) Fenner, was born in the Township of Gunplain, Allegan County, Mich., October 23, 1878, and October 28, 1896, married David Edward Brown, son of Henry and Jane (Wood) Brown. He was born in Gunplain Township, Mich., October 27, 1874.

Children:—

259 I. Verne LeRoy, born in Gunplain, October 10, 1899.

260 II. Reon David, born in Gunplain, February 23, 1904.

261 III. Iola May, born in Gunplain, August 28, 1909.

Edith May (Fenner) Brown (147): Address, Plainwell, Mich.

148. Ida Myrtle Fenner, IX., daughter of Franklin Monroe (53) and Hannah Ida (Honeysett) Fenner, was born in Gunplain Township, Allegan County, Mich., July 17, 1880, and February 4, 1901, married Boaz Camfield, son of Boaz and Anna (Bellingham) Camfield. He was born at Rotherfield, Sussex, England, October 11, 1872.

Children:—

262 I. Nordah Lavee, born in Gunplain, Allegan County, Mich., October 4, 1902.

263 II. Franklin Boaz, born in Gunplain, Allegan County, Mich., June 18, 1905.

Ida Myrtle (Fenner) Camfield (148): Address, Plainwell, Mich.

149. Starr Franklin Fenner, IX., son of Franklin Monroe (53) and Hannah Ida (Honeysett) Fenner, was born in Gunplain, Allegan County, Mich., February 24, 1886, and February 24, 1910, married Frances M. Greene, daughter of Abner and Marion D. (Root) Greene. She was born at Kendalls, Mich., May 23, 1891.

Starr Franklin Fenner (149): Address, Plainwell, Mich.

152. Nellie Maria Schenck, IX., daughter of Hulbert Luke (54) and Betsey (Fenner) Schenck, was born in Lysander Township, Onondaga County, N. Y., September 11, 1867, and November 6, 1890, married Edmund Harvey Turner, son of Samuel and Ellen (Mills) Turner. He was born in Lysander Township, January 24, 1866.

Children:—

264 I. Hattie Betsey was born in Lysander Township, June 10, 1891, and died August 3, 1903.

265 II. Anna Nellie, born in Lysander Township, May 18, 1900.

266 III. Ellen May, born in Lysander Township, September 14, 1901.

Nellie M. (Schenck) Turner (152): Address, R. F. D., Memphis, N. Y.

153. William Vanderveer Schenck, IX., son of Hulbert Luke (54) and Betsey (Fenner) Schenck, was born in Lysander Township, Onondaga County, N. Y., January 22, 1875, and December 1, 1895, married Nellie Wright, daughter of Charles and Caroline (Miller) Wright. She was born in Ira, Cayuga County, N. Y., March 22, 1874.

Children:—

267 I. John Hulbert, born in Lysander Township, February 3, 1900.

268 II. Lillian May, born in Lysander Township, July 9, 1909.

William Vanderveer Schenck (153): Address, R. F. D., Memphis, N. Y.

154. Lester Hulbert Schenck, IX., son of James Shuler (56) and Ella Lucretia (Wormuth) Schenck, was born in Lysander Township, Onondaga County, N. Y., August 4, 1880, and October 21, 1903, married Thola Nett Tabor, daughter of Ernest Grant and Nett (Clark) Tabor. She was born in the Township of Cato, Cayuga County, N. Y., August 16, 1885.

Lester Hulbert Schenck (154): Address, R. F. D., Memphis, N. Y.

158. Elva Simmons, IX., daughter of George William and Effie Isadore (Schenck) Simmons (60), was born in Lysander Township, Onondaga County, N. Y., August 31, 1871, and September 4, 1895, married Edward Bela Kaple, son of Dr. John Delmar and Martha (Goodrich) Kaple. He was born at Hartwich, N. Y., March 1, 1872.

Elva (Simmons) Kaple (158): Address, Elbridge, N. Y.

160. Florence Loretta Schenck, IX., daughter of William Baird (61) and Florence Loretta (Osborn) Schenck, was born in Lysander Township, Onondaga County, N. Y., August 3, 1880, and October 5, 1898, married Ceylon Charles Shearer, son of William Charles and Ann (Murray) Shearer. He was born at Homer, N. Y., January 5, 1872.

Children:—

269 I. Alice Loretta, born at Homer, N. Y., September 2, 1900.
270 II. Grace Reba, born at Cortland, N. Y., December 22, 1902.
271 III. Marion Nellie, born at Cortland, N. Y., August 11, 1904.
272 IV. Neva Estella, born at Cortland, N. Y., December 19, 1908.

Florence Loretta (Schenck) Shearer (160): Address, 3 Wadsworth St., Cortland, N. Y.

161. Rulef David Schenck, IX., son of William Beard (61) and Florence Loretta (Osborn) Schenck, was born in Lysander Township, Onondaga County, N. Y., January 21, 1885, and September 6, 1905, married

Irma Louise Givens, daughter of George E. and Hattie (Harter) Givens. She was born at Ithaca, N. Y., October 2, 1884.

Children:—

    273 I. Lawrence David, born at Cortland, N. Y., December 12, 1906.

    274 II. Luthera Jane, born at Cortland, N. Y., May 6, 1910.

Rulef David Schenck (161): Address, 92 Lincoln Av., Cortland, N. Y.

TENTH GENERATION IN AMERICA.

162. Ada Mary Wilson, X., daughter of Mervin James (62) and Cornelia (Harrington) Wilson, was born at Memphis, Onondaga County, N. Y., January 1, 1881, and March 12, 1902, married Frederick W. Corey, son of Charles H. and Helen (Knight) Corey. He was born at Jordan, N. Y., July 5, 1873.

Children:—

    275 I. Eunice Catherine was born at Syracuse, N. Y., July 15, 1903, and died there April 18, 1904.

Ada M. (Wilson) Corey (162): Address, 919 W. Onondaga St., Syracuse, N. Y.

163. Willard Dennis Stone, X., son of Delancy Duyane and Orinda More (Wilson) Stone (63), was born in Lysander Township, Onondaga County, N. Y., June 7, 1870, and February 12, 1894, married Hilda Norman, daughter of Olif Norman. She was born July 9, 1871.

They had two children:—

    276 I. Norman D., born at Baldwinsville, N. Y., November 1, 1894.

    277 II. Donald D., born at Baldwinsville, N. Y., December 13, 1895.

Willard Dennis Stone (163) married again, February, 1904, Eunice Howe. His address is Cato, N. Y.

164. Rosa Anna Stone, X., daughter of Delancy Duyane and Orinda More (Wilson) Stone (63), was born in Lysander Township, Onondaga County., N. Y., October 5, 1879, and April 3, 1907, married Dr. William T. Hudson, son of Watson N. and Mary (French) Hudson. He was born at Auburn, N. Y., July 6, 1874.

Rosa Anna (Stone) Hudson (164): Address, Auburn, N. Y.

168. Harriet Belle Lowe, X., daughter of Joseph Garret and Inez Ann (Vedder) Lowe (70), was born at Washington, Kas., June 23, 1874, and January 22, 1903, married Frederic Tobey Stackpole, son of Frederic W. and S. Elizabeth (Tobey) Stackpole. He was born at Thomastown, Me., November 18, 1874.

Children:—

278 I. Joseph Frederic, born at Seattle, Wash., April 14, 1904.
279 II. Frederic Tobey, born at El Reno, Okla., December 23, 1908.

Harriet Belle (Lowe) Stackpole (168): Address, El Reno, Okla.

169. Russell Gordon Lowe, X., son of Joseph Garret and Inez Ann (Vedder) Lowe (70), was born at Washington, Kas., November 12, 1877, and July 4, 1901, married Doris Pearl Carlock, daughter of Andrew Means and Luella (Cullom) Carlock. She was born at Cleburne, Tex., April 26, 1879.

Children:—

280　I.　Helen Marjorie, born at Perry, Okla., June 25, 1902.
281　II.　Gordon Cullom, born at Perry, Okla., March 11, 1906.

Russell Gordon Lowe (169): Address, Oklahoma City, Okla.

170.　Clara Leslie Lowe, X., daughter of Joseph Garret and Inez Ann (Vedder) Lowe (70), was born at Washington, Kas., May 31, 1880, and October 12, 1904, married Dr. Ralph Evans Runkle, son of Winfield S. and Mirium (Evans) Runkle. He was born at Mingo, O., February 26, 1878.

Children:—

282　I.　Winfield Lowe, born at El Reno, Okla, June 22, 1908.

Clara Leslie (Lowe) Runkle (170): Address, El Reno, Okla.

176.　Maud May Hallowell, X., daughter of Alfred Mortimer and Harriet Elnora (Vedder) Hallowell (71) was born at Washington, Kas., April 13, 1876, and June 30, 1894, married Claude Clinton Needham, son of Nathan B. and Mary A. (Graves) Needham. He was born at Clifton, Kas., May 7, 1876.

Children:—

283　I.　Claude Raymond, born at El Reno, Okla., June 18, 1899.

Maud May (Hallowell) Needham (176): Address, Ventura, Cal.

188.　Jessie Belle Bratt, X., daughter of Charles Willis (84) and Nettie Matilda (Horton) Bratt, was born at Plainville, Onondaga County, N. Y., May 2,

1884, and December 24, 1903, married Earl Lewis Johnson, son of George H. and Emily (Lewis) Johnson. He was born at Granby, N. Y., August 21, 1883.

Children:—

284 I. Lela Bratt, born at Fulton, N. Y., January 14, 1907.
285 II. Kenneth Charles, born at Fulton, N. Y., September 9, 1908.

Jessie Belle (Bratt) Johnson (188): Address, 407 Wilbur Ave., Syracuse, N. Y.

190. Hattie May Vanderveer, X., daughter of Garret L. and Ella May (Bratt) Vanderveer (85), was born at Plainville, N. Y., October 5, 1881, and November 22, 1899, married Charles Theodore Lange, son ot Frederick and Elizabeth (Kwitz) Lange. He was born at South Granby, Oswego County, N. Y., June 18, 1881.

Children:—

286 I. Raymond Charles, born at South Grandy, N. Y., April 30, 1901.
287 II. Ernest William, born at South Granby, N. Y., July 5, 1904.

Hattie May (Vanderveer) Lange (190): Address, South Granby, N. Y.

202. Avis May Carncross, X., daughter of Miles Clarence and Ella Lillian (Hubbard) Carncross (90), was born at Meridian, Cayuga County, N. Y., January 31, 1884, and December 14, 1905, married Charles Egbert Cox, son of William B. and Mary Frances (Gordon) Cox. He was born at Hortontown, Onondaga County, N. Y., December 27, 1879.

Children:—

288 I. Maurice Egbert, born at Syracuse, N. Y., July 9, 1908.

Avis May (Carncross) Cox (202): Address, 219 West Corning Av., Syracuse, N. Y.

215. Harry Barrett Phelps, X., son of Louis Spaulding (112) and Carrie M. (Barnard) Phelps, was born at Granby, Oswego County, N. Y., August 9, 1886, and February 4, 1905, married Harriet L. Osborn.

Harry Barrett Phelps (215): Address, United States Navy, Washington, D. C.

216. Homer Spaulding Phelps, X., son of Louis Spaulding (112) and Carrie M. (Barnard) Phelps, was born at Granby, Oswego County, N. Y., April 11, 1888, and June 26, 1907, married Nellie Mae Wolcott, daughter of John and Elizabeth Mae (Tillapaugh) Wolcott. She was born at Pulaski, N. Y., May 8, 1889.

Children:—
> 289 I. Lena Mae was born at Fulton, N. Y., February 17, 1908, and died there October 7, 1908.

Homer Spaulding Phelps (216): Address, 423 Columbia St., Utica, N. Y.

242. Maude Belle Scott, X., daughter of William Henry (133) and Alice Belle (Phillips) Scott, was born at Ludington, Mich., September 28, 1883, and January 28, 1910, married William Howard Rice, son of William L. and Emily Ann (Corsin) Rice. He was born at Mendon, Mich., August 13, 1884.

Maude Belle (Scott) Rice (242): Address, 713 Southworth Place, Kalamazoo, Mich.

243. Harry Agatha Scott, X., son of William Henry (133) and Allie Belle (Phillips) Scott, was born at Plainwell, Mich., November 25, 1889, and July 14, 1909, married Bessie Lenora Lum, daughter of Harrison V. and Harriet Emeline (Brininstool) Lum. She was born at Galesburg, Kalamazoo County, Mich., December 20, 1884.

Harry Agatha Scott (243):—Address, 1521 Fairbanks Court, Kalamazoo, Mich.

INDEX

Adams, Amos 45
    Marvin 45
Adsit, Elon Bratt (201) 109
    Francis 109
    Franklin Mills 109
    Sarah Bratt (89) 85-109
Afferden, Lord of 23, 24, 25 55, 56, 57
Albright, Anna Bratt (86) 85-108
    Charles Wesley (193) 108
    Henry Clay (196) 108
    Howard Baxter (194) 108
    Jacob 108
    John Wesley 108
    Wesley Alfred (195) 108
Allis, T. W. 72
American History, Early 27
Amersfoort (Flatlands, L. I.) 28-29
Amsden, Harriet 118
Arssen, Lord of 56
Babcock, David 106
    Ella 106
    Margaret 106
Baird, Caroline 65
    Elsie 43-65
    Family, Note on 43
    John 43
    William 65

Baker, Mary J. 104
Baldwin, Dr. James C. 44
Baldwin's Bridge, N. Y. 44
Baldwinsville, N. Y. 44
"Baldwinsville Gazette" 44
"Baldwinsville Republican" 44
Barber, Addie E. 93
Barnard, Carrie M. 113
    Selah Smith 113
Bates, Deborah 82
    James 82
    Louisa Wilson (19) 66-82
    Samuel W. 82
Bellingham, Anna 123
Bertholf, Rev. Guillaume 38
Betts, Chauncey 45-52
Betts' Corners, N. Y. 45
Bittel, Elizabeth 112
Blyenbeck, Castle of 24, 25, 26, 28, 56, 57
Bout, Jan Everston 28
Bowman, Maude 111
    Willis 111
Bradt, See note 86
Bratt, Alice Merriman (87) 85, 108
    Alice Viola (200) 109
    Anna Isabel (86) 85, 108
    Arthur (99) 87, 111
    Charles Willis (84) 85, 107
    Earl (204) 110
    Edith (209) 110
    Ella May (85) 85, 107
    Eliza Ann (31) 70
    Elsie (33) 70, 85
    Ernest Wilson (88) 85, 109
    Ethel (208) 110
    Florence Louise (210) 111
    Florence May (199) 109
    Frances (206) 110

Bratt, Frank Leslie (83) 85, 106
   Glenn (205) 110
   Gertrude Ruth (211) 111
   Harry (101) 87, 111
   Herbert Eugene (97)................................ 87, 110
   Jessie Belle (188) 107, 128
   John 45, 48, 70
   John (32) 70, 85
   Lela Jane (189) 107
   LeRoy (98) 87, 110
   Mabel (207) 110
   Margaret Schenck (5) 48, 65, 70
   Peter 48, 70
   Peter Schenck (35) 70, 86
   Raymond (102) 87, 112
   Rebecca 70
   Ruth (103) 87
   Sarah Catharine (34) 48, 70, 82, 86
   Sarah Elsie (89) 85, 109
   William Peter (100) 87, 111
Brininstool, Harriet Emeline 131
Brinkerhoff, Susanna Abrahamse 61
Brown, David Edward 122
   Edith Fenner (147) 97, 122
   Henry 122
   Iola May (261) 123
   John 36
   Reon David (260) 122
   Verne Le Roy (259) 122
Brugers, Gertgen 25, 26
Buchanan, Emma 121
Buck, John 45, 48
Buel, Grover 45
Bullock, Caroline Scott (139) 96, 120
   Ira 120
   Ira R. 120
Bump, W. P. 45
Burke, Anna 105

Burrows, Jennie Lavinia 120
Burtnett, Charles Gordon 103
    Harriet Vedder (71) 83, 102
Camfield, Boas 123
    Franklin Boas (263) 123
    Ida Fenner (148) 97, 123
    Nordah Lavee (262) 123
Cannedy, Lucy 116
Carlock, Andrew Means 127
    Doris Pearl 127
Carncross, Avis Mav (202) 110, 129
    Ella Hubbard (90) 86, 109
    Frank Hubbard (203) 110
    John 109
    Miles Clarence 109
Carpenter, George 86
    Marta Nettie 86
    Ruth 86
Carroll, David 45, 47
Carson, Frances 110
Case, Mary Elizabeth 96
    Sarah 96
    Stephen 96
Cayuga County, Branch of Family in 42, 64
Ceathoat, Isadora 114
Chapman, Adelia 92
    Austin 92
    Delia Spaulding (42) 74, 92
    Earl Burns (115) 93, 114
    Hazel Eliza (116) 93, 114
    Irwin B. (114) 93
    L. Austin 92
    Minnie Geraldine (226) 114
Charlemagne 19
Charles V., Emperor 26, 27
Charles the Simple 19
Charleston, N. Y. 41, 46
Chase, Cecile Caroline (241) 118

Chase, Elliott Leo (240) 118
    Herbert Fenner (238) 118
    Hiram 118
    Jennie Fenner (129) 95, 118
    Manley Maurice 118
    Maurice Manley (239) 118
Chittenden, Ella Eliza 84
    Samuel Mallory 84
Christian Church at Plainville 45
Clark, Mary 108
    Nett 124
Cleve, Duke of 23
    Governor 30
Coat of Arms 13
Coats, Benjamin 81
    Charlotte Wilson (15) 66, 67, 81
Cogswell, Frances 84
Colburn, Rev. E. E. 69
Columbia, N. Y. 44
Conover, Garret 63
Corey, Ada Wilson (162) 100, 126
    Charles H. 126
    Eunice Catherine (275) 126
    Frederick W. 126
Corsin, Emily Ann 130
Cox, Avis Carncross (202) 110, 129
    Charles Egbert 129
    Maurice Egbert (288) 129
    William B. 129
Cradenborch, House at 25
Crigers, Catrina 31, 62
Cullum, Luella 127
Custers, Alheit 25, 26, 57, 59
Dailey, Abram 45, 48
Davis, B. F. 48
Day, Adaline 83, 94
    Eliza Ann 83, 94
    Eliza 94

Day, Hezekiah 83, 94
de Haes, Marie Magdalena 59
de Hart 63
de Witte, Colve 20
Doane, Adelbert 111
    Iona Leona 111
Dunham, Joseph 103
    Sardis A. 103
Dunsmore, Almeron Ward 113
    Inez Spaulding (110) 92, 112
    Phineas H. 113
Dutcher, Daniel 49
Eddy, Ernestine Adele 103
    Lucien Crane 103
Eesley, Albert 119
    Franklin R. B. (246) 119
    Harold John (245) 119
    Iva Belle (244) 119
    John Franklin 119
    Kittie Scott (134) 95, 119
Elder, Theresa M. 98
Elser, Florence 105
    John Joshua 105
Elsworth, Mary Ann 109
Emerick, Abraham 49, 80
    Emerancy 50, 80
Erickson, Axel Walfred 105
    Erik Axel 105
    Harriet Smith (79) 84, 105
Ensign, Josephine 120
Evans, Mirium 128
Farley, Alice 111
Farmersville, N. Y. 45
Faulkner, Nancy 68
Fenner, Arthur, Capt. 74
    Avis, Melissa (45) 75
    Betsey 97
    Betsey Perry 75, 77

Fenner, Byron Nash (128) 95
    Byron Nichols (254) 121
    Byron Russell (49) 77, 95
    Charles Day (126) 94, 117
    Clay Earl (150) 97
    Dorothy Isabella (258) 122
    Edith May (147) 97, 122
    Eleanor Schenck (9) 50, 65, 66, 74, 76
    Eliza Eleanor (50) 77, 95
    Elton Perry (146) 97
    Ernest William (140) 96, 121
    Florence Ellen (118) 93, 115
    Frank Clifton (230) 115
    Franklin Eddy (48) 75
    Franklin Monroe (53) 77, 97
    Frederick Byron (43) 75
    Frederick Munroe (228) 115
    Frederick W. 50, 74, 97
    Frederick William (47) 75, 94
    Frederick William (127) 94, 117
    Gerald James (257) 122
    Gertrude Helen (256) 122
    Halcyon Edith (237) 118
    Hannah Jane (143) 96
    Hannah Schenck (10) 50, 65, 71, 76
    Harry Rulef (229) 115
    Helen Angeline (253) 121
    Horace Alfred (252) 121
    Ida Myrtle (148) 97, 123
    James Bruce (142) 96, 121
    James Emory (117) 93, 115
    James L. 50, 75, 77
    James Rulef (44) 75, 93
    Jennie (129) 95, 118
    John 97
    Lucinda T. 74
    Nellie May (141) 96, 121
    Nina Vanderveer (131) 95

Fenner, Orlie Perry (145) 96, 122
    Pearl Eliza (144) 96
    Raymond Erasmus (231) 115
    Rulef James (52) 77, 96
    Russell B. 50, 77, 97
    Russell William (255) 122
    Sarah Ellen (46) 75, 93
    Starr Franklin (149) 97, 123
    Wave Iola (151) 97
    William Perry (51) 77, 96
    William Perry (130) 95
Finley, Elizabeth 105
Fishback, Frances 116
Fisher, Mary 106
Fitzgerald, Daniel James 91
    Henrietta Schenck (38) 71, 91
    John 91
    Nancy 91
Forncrook, Stuffle 52
French, Mary 127
Gaesdonk, Convent of 23, 24, 25
Galloway, Florence Fenner (118) 93, 115
    Frederick Thomas 115
    Henry 115
    Wilbur Fenner (232) 115
Geldern, Bailiff of 24
Geyen, Church of 22
Gibberfort, Bailiff of 57
Gibbs, Augusta 111
    Grace Edna 111
    William 111
Givens, George E. 126
    Irma Louise 126
Goldie, Jennette 119
Goodman, Sarah Ellen 113
Goodrich, Martha 125
Gordon, Mary Frances 129
Gorham, Freeman 68

Gorham, Parna Sullivan 49, 68
Graves, Mary A. 128
Greene, Abner 123
    Francis M. 123
Greenfield, Mary A. 103
Grimes, Rev. W. J. 69
Groff, Abigail Ann 104
Haeghoort, Rev. Gerardus 38
Haes, Godart 25
Hall, Grace 110
    Julia Parsels 49, 68
    Mary 43
    Robert 110
Hallowell, Alfred Mortimer 102
    Edith Leona (179) 103
    Harriet Vedder (71) 83, 102
    Henry Raymond (178) 102
    Jesse R. 102
    Lyman Earl (180) 103
    Maud May (176) 102, 128
    Penelope A. 102
    Roscoe Vedder (177) 102
Hammond, Frances E. 110
    George 110
    Hettie 110
Hankenson, James 64
Harrington, Catherine 100
    Cornelia 100
    Thomas 100
Hazengest, Estate of 25
Hegeman, Isaac 61
Hendrickson, Geesie 63
Henry the Fowler 19
Hicks, Elizabeth 96
Hill, Harvey Cooney 105
    Loula Anna 105
Hillenrath, Heiress of 56
Hinsdell, Eleanor Schenck (9) 50, 65, 66, 74, 76

Hinsdell, Perry H. 50, 75
Hitchcock, Harriet E. 115
Holden, Sarah 118
Holland History 17
Holmes, Katherine 63
Holton, Suel 51
Honeysett, Hannah 97
 Hannah Ida 97
 James 97
Horst, Lord of 56
Horton Edward 107
 Mary 107
 Nettie Matilda 107
Hosmer, C. M. 44
Howe, Eunice 127
 Joseph 47
Hubbard Chauncey 85
 Cornelius 52
 Elijah 85
 Eliza 85
 Elsie Bratt (33) 70, 85
 Ella Lillian (90) 86, 109
Hudson, Rosa Stone (164) 100, 127
 Watson N. 127
 William T. 127
Humphrey, Hattie Osborn 107
Hunt, John 81
Huntington, Elsie Schenck (82) 85, 106
 Frederick L. 106
 Henry L. 106
 Lisle Schenck (187) 106
Hydorn, Caroline 120
Irish, Louise B. 81
Jackson, Alice Bratt (87) 85, 108
 Edward Alexander 108
 Eyola Bratt (197) 108
 Reba Mary (198) 108
 Richard 108

Johnson, Earl Lewis 129
   George H. 129
   Jessie Bratt (188) 107, 128
   Kenneth Charles (285) 129
   Lela Bratt (284) 129
Jones, Leida 93
Jonson, Hedda Louise 105
Kaple, Edward Bela 125
   Elva Simmons (158) 99, 125
   John Delmar 125
Keller, James 117
   Mabel 117
Kelly, Jessie Mead 117
Kennedy, Amy 103
   Dennis 51
Kerpen, Monastery of 22
Ketchum, Fernando 122
   Harry Albertus 114
   Hazel Chapman (116) 93, 114
   Isabella 122
   James Robert 114
   Robert Burns (227) 114
Kinch, John A. 104
   Kathryn Augusta (185) 104
   Nellie Smith (76) 84, 104
   Samuel R. 104
Knight, Helen 126
Kwitz, Elizabeth 129
Kyle, Alexander 112
   Caroline A. 112
   Caroline Inez (214) 112
   Charles Watson 112
   Inez Spaulding (110) 92, 112
Landiss, Ella 117
Lange, Charles Theodore 129
   Ernest Wililam (287) 129
   Frederick 129
   Hattie Vanderveer (190) 107, 129

Lange, Raymond Charles (286) 129
Larabee, Alice 104
Lewis, Emily 129
Lindsay, Lillian 103
Lippert, Sarah 41, 64
Locke, Ann 100
    John V. N. 100
    Minnie Ann 100
Loet, Estate of 57
Lowe, Ausborn E. 102
    Bessie Inez (173) 102
    Clara Leslie (170) 102, 128
    Gordon Cullom (281) 128
    Harriet Belle (168) 102, 127
    Helen Marjorie (280) 128
    Inez Vedder (70) 83, 101
    Joseph Garret 102
    Joseph Garret (171) 102
    Mildred Adeline (174) 102
    Richard Vedder (172) 102
    Russell Gordon (169) 102, 127
    Ruth Marjorie (175) 102
    Sarah J. 102
Lum, Bessie Lenora 131
    Harrison V. 131
Lysander, N. Y. 45
    Early settlers of 45
    Pioneer days of.. 46
McCallum, Jessie Jane 112
    Peter 112
McColl, Bertha Scott (138) 96, 120
    John Samuel 120
    John Thomas 120
McIndoe, Agnes 112
McKinney, Ellen 114
McLean, Isabella 120
Marlborough, Old Brick Church of 39
Martin, Margaret 117

Mastin, Allen Snyder 103
    Olive 103
Miller, Albert 107
    Caroline 124
    Lillian 107
    Mary 107
Mills, Ellen 123
    Mary 109
Moerschler, Anna Cornelia 101
    John 101
Monfoort, Anna 56
Morgan, Rev. Joseph 38
Motley 18, 26
Moulton, Belle A. 119
    Irvin L. 119
Mount, Cornelius 52
Munster Mannshof 23
Murray, Ann 125
Mylligen, Estate of 57
Nash, Caroline V. 95
    Major D. 95
    Phoebe 95
Navasink, Church of 37, 38
Needham, Claude Clinton 128
    Claude Raymond (283) 128
    Maud Hallowell (176) 102, 128
    Nathan B. 128
Nefus, Peter 61
Netherlands, History of 17
Nichols, George 121
    Grace 121
Nicoll, Gov. Richard 29
Norman, Hilda 126
    Olif 126
Norton, Ann 91
    Ann (109) 91
    Georgianna Belle (107) 91
    Harriet Maria (108) 91

Norton, Henrietta Schenck (38) 71, 91
    John Vedder 91, 94
    Lyman 45, 48, 91
Notter, John A. 119
    Maud May 119
Nulty, Caroline 101
Nydeggen, Castle of 16, 21
Nyfterich, Estate of 57
Onondaga County, N. Y. 44, 46
Osborn, David 99
    Florence Loretta 99
    Harriet L. 130
    Margaret Ann 99
Ostrander, Sarah Agnes 113
    William Henry 113
Otis, Margaret 106
Ottersum, Estate at 24
Pangburn, Herman 49
Parish, Julia Eliza 84
Parker, Melissa 113
Parma, Prince of 27
Pease, Caroline 117
Perkins, Annie Spaulding (41) 74, 92
    Erastus B. 92
    J. Edward 92
    Sarah 92
Perry, Samuel 50
Peters, Lucy Juliette 113
Phelps, Alfred (224) 114
    Anna Laura (220) 114
    Caroline A. 91
    Eliza Eleanor (218) 113
    Gertrude (222) 114
    H. Nelson 91, 92
    Harold Major (219) 113
    Harry Barrett (215) 113, 130
    Homer Jay (113) 92, 113
    Homer Spaulding (216) 113, 130

Phelps, Lena Mae (289) 130
    Lena Marion (217) 113
    Louis Spaulding (112) 92, 113
    Major Fitts 92
    Mary 91, 92
    Mary Spaulding (40) 74, 92
    Mildred Bessie (221) 114
    Raymond Lee (223) 114
    Ruth Marjorie (225) 114
Phillips, Albert 118
    Allie Belle 118
Pincerna, Christianus 16
Pinckney, Alpheus 115
    Julia 115
    Lou A. 115
Plainville, N. Y. 44
    Early Settlers of 45
    Christian Church at 45
    First School at 45
Pleasant Valley, N. J. 36, 41
Pomeroy, Clara Lelia (155) 99
    Edgar Schenck (156) 99
    Lelia Schenck 79, 98
    Harry Eltweed (157) 99
    T. Edgar 98
    Theodore C. 98
Pratt, Frank A. 121
    Nellie Fenner (141) 92, 121
    William 121
Presley, Roxie 122
Preston, Northrup 51
Quackenbush, Mary 64
Ransom, Fannie Elizabeth 120
    John Noyes 120
Reed, Eliza 108
Rice, Maud Scott (242) 118, 130
    William Howard 130
    William L. 130

Robinson, Harriet Parthenia 87
    Horatio N. 87
Rogers, Frank Adelbert 112
    Martha Jessie 112
Romain, Jacobus 38
Root, Marion D. 123
Rumrill, Edna 117
    Edward 117
Runkle, Clara Lowe (170) 102, 128
    Ralph Evans 128
    Winfield Lowe (282) 128
    Winfield S. 128
Rutgen, Catherine 25
Savage, Ellen A. 93
    Emily 93
    Seth 93
Sayles, Major 49
Schall, Ephraim 114
    Minnie Mae 114
Schenck, Adrian Adelbert (37) 5, 9, 71, 87
    Alexander D. 6, 15, 21, 37
    Alice Maladine (59) 80
    Alchy (16a) 63
    Ann (15a) 63
    Ann Tator (64) 82, 98, 101
    Anetje (3a) 61
    Benjamin Baird (6) 45, 46, 65, 70, 72
    Benjamin Freeman (30) 68, 84
    Benjamin Robinson (105) 87, 112
    Benjamin Rush (36) 70
    Catharine (4) 51, 65
    Catharine (23a) 63
    Cornelius (28a) 41, 64
    Daniel 64
    Derivation of Name of 14
    Effie Isadore (60) 80, 99
    Eleanor (9) 50, 65, 66, 74, 76
    Eleanor (25a) 63

Schenck, Eleanor (30a) 64
    Eliza (7) 52, 65, 66, 74
    Elsie (23) 67
    Elsie (104) 87
    Elsie May (82) 85, 106
    Florence Loretta (160) 100, 125
    Floyd Sullivan (74) 84, 103
    Frederick Tyler (106) 87
    Fredericus 21
    Garret (7a) 36, 37, 38, 61
    Garret C. 6
    Gasha (29a) 64
    Gasha (31a) 64
    Gerret Roelofse (7a) 36, 37, 38, 61
    Hannah V. (10) 50, 65, 71, 76
    Harriet Livonia (25) 67, 83
    Hendrick (26a) 63
    Henrietta Maria (38) 71, 91
    Hermanus 21
    Hulbert Luke (54) 79, 97
    Irwin Vanderveer (55) 79, 98
    Jan (6a) 36, 37, 38, 61, 62
    Jane (21a) 63
    James F. 37
    James Harvey (26) 68
    James L. (12) 49, 51, 65, 79
    James Shuler (56) 79, 98
    James Warren (57) 79
    Johannes 7, 59, 60
    John (3) 46, 65, 67
    John (14a) 63
    John (24a) 40, 63
    John (32a) 64
    John Hulbert (267) 124
    John Sullivan (27) 68, 83
    John Tyler (213) 112
    Jonica (4a) 61
    Julia (80) 85

Schenck, Lawrence David (273) 126

Leah (20a) 63

Leila Marion (212) 112

Lelia Maria (58) 79, 98

Lester Hulbert (154) 98, 124

Lillian May (268) 124

Lisle John (81) 85, 106

Luthera Jane (274) 126

Margaret (5) 48, 65, 70

Margaret (34a) 64

Margaretta (8a) 36, 62

Maria (17a) 63

Marike (5a) 61

Martin (2a) 61

Mary (33a) 64

Mayke (10a) 62

Michael 59

Mildred Louise (181) 103

Moses 64

Nancy Theresa (28) 68

Neeltje (9a) 36, 62

Nellie Maria (152) 97, 123

Nellie (19a) 63

Parna Eleanora (24) 48, 67, 82

P. L. 7

Perlina Adele (29) 68, 84

Peter (13a) 62

Reynier 21

Roelof (12a) 37, 38, 39, 62, 63

Epitaph of 40

Roelof Martense (36A-1a) 27, 28, 55, 58, 61, 62

valuation of property of 30

marriage contract of 31

will of 33

Robert C. 37

Rulef (35a-1) 42, 45, 64, 65

Rulef (13) 47, 50, 65, 80

Schenck, Rulef David (161) 100, 125
 Rulief (27a) 41, 64
 Rulief 2nd 64
 Sally (2) 47, 65, 66, 85
 Sara (11a) 62
 Sarah (18a) 63
 Sarah (22a) 63
 Theodorus 21
 Willaim 21
 Willem 21
 William, Rev. 6, 37, 61
 William Baird (11) 52, 65, 78
 William Baird (61) 80, 99
 William C. 37
 William R. 37
 William Vanderveer (153) 97, 124
 Woodhull S. 37
Schenck van Nydeck, Adelheid 25
 Adelheid (25A) 57
 Alheid (16A) 57
 Alheit (7A) 56
 Anetje (38A) 28, 55, 58
 Anna (17A) 57
 Arnold 56
 Christianus 21, 22
 Christoffle 27
 Dederick (28A) 57, 58
 Derick (11A) 25, 56, 57, 59
 Derick (20A) 57, 59
 Diederich (5A) 25, 56, 57
 Heinrich (1A) 17, 23, 55, 56
 Heinrich (3A) 23, 24, 55, 56
 Heinrich (12A) 56
 Heinrich (22A) 57
 Jan (37A) 28, 55, 58
 Johann (6A) 56
 Johann (9A) 56

Schenck van Nydeck, Johann (23A) 57
    Johann (31A) 58
    Lisbeth (4A) 23, 56
    Lisbeth (18A) 57
    Margaretha (27A) 57
    Maria (26A) 57
    Maria Margaretha (32A) 58
    Maria Magdelina (33A) 58
    Martin (29A) 26, 28, 58
    Martin (35A) 27, 58, 59
    Otto (14A) 56
    Otto (19A) 57
    Peter (21A) 57, 59
    Peter (30A) 27, 28, 58
    Petronella (13A) 25, 56
    Roelmann (10A) 56
    Roelof Martense (36A-1a).......................27, 28, 55, 58, 61, 62
    Thomas (15A) 57
    Wilhelmina (34A) 58
    Wilhelmus 22
    Winand (8A) 25, 56
    Winand (24A) 57
    Wynand (2A) 23, 24, 55
Schuyler, John P. 50
Scofield, A. B. 45
    Elias 45
Scott, Bertha May (138) 96, 120
    Captain 29
    Caroline Eleanor (139) 96, 120
    Charles Seneca (135) 95, 119
    Donald Notter (249) 120
    Dorothea Moulton (247) 119
    Eliza Fenner (50) 77, 95
    Franklin James (137) 96, 120
    Gerald Notter (251) 120
    Harry Agatha (243) 118, 131
    Henry Robley 95

Scott, Herbert Russell (136) 95, 119
 Herbert Russell (248) 120
 Ira 95
 Kittie Belle (134) 95, 119
 Mary B. 95
 Mary Eleanor (132) 95
 Maude Belle (242) 118, 130
 Nathan Burrows (250) 120
 William Henry (133) 95, 118
Seipmacher 13, 22
Servoss, Daniel 51
Shearer, Alice Loretta (269) 125
 Ceylon Charles 125
 Florence Schenck (160) 100, 125
 Grace Reba (270) 125
 Marion Nellie (271) 125
 Neva Estella (272) 125
 William Charles 125
Sheldon, Ralph 101
Shepard, Polly 47
Simmons, Effie Schenck (60) 80, 99
 Elizabeth 99
 Elva (158) 99, 125
 George William 99
 Peter 99
 Raymond Percy (159) 99
Skinner, Joseph H. 72
Smith, Alfred 45
 Charles 84
 Charles Elser (186) 105
 Charles Fred (75) 84, 104
 Elizabeth Gertrude (182) 104
 Frances Cogswell 83
 Garner 50
 Harry James (78) 84, 105
 Harriet Marie (79) 84, 105
 Joseph Lowe (77) 84, 105

Smith, Josiah 51
   Nellie Leslie (76) 84, 104
   Perlina Schenck (29) 68, 84
   Richard 45, 51, 84
   Sophia C. 84
   Stevens 84
Snow, Elijah 48
   Eunice 80
Sornbury, Horace 96
   Mina L. 96
Spaulding, Annie Laura (41) 74, 02
   Burns (39) 74, 91
   Dealia (42) 74, 92
   Eliza Schenck (7) 52, 65, 66, 74
   Inez Eudora (110) 92-112
   Irving Burns (111) 92
   Mary 74
   Mary C. (40) 74, 92
   Solomon B. 52, 74
Springport, N. Y. 42
Springport, N. Y., Branch of Family.......................... 64
Stackpole, Frederic Tobey 127
   Frederic Tobey (279) 127
   Frederic W. 127
   Harriet Lowe (168) 102, 127
   Joseph Frederic (278) 127
Stayman, William D. 121
   Wilma Belle 121
Stek, Count Goessen 25
Stevens, Benjamin 50
   Eleanor 109
   John 109
   Julia 109
Stickle, Elizabeth 106
   Jacob 106
   Jennie 106
Stoddard, Mr. 45, 48

Stone, Alpheus 100
    Donald D. (277) 126
    Dulancy Duyane 100
    Jennie Lucy (165) 100
    Lucy Ann 100
    Norman D. (276) 126
    Orinda Wilson (63) 81, 100
    Rosa Anna (164) 100, 127
    Willard Dennis (163) 100, 126
Straden, Mayor of 56
Sullivan, Bonapart 73
    Harriet 49, 70
    John 68
    Nancy 67, 68, 70, 79
    Nancy Maria 49, 79
    Parna 49, 68
    Perlina 49, 67, 68
    Richard 49, 67, 68, 70, 79
    Sybal 68
Swaney, Mary J. 121
Tabor, Ernest Grant 124
    Thola Nett 124
Tator, Ann L. 51, 79, 81
    Ann Hubble (64) 82, 98, 101
    Charlotte Wilson (15) 66, 67, 81
    Frederick I. 51, 79, 81
    James M. 81, 98
    Jane Wilson (17) 66, 67, 81, 98
    Jehial E. 81
    Lydia Amanda 81
    Polly 79, 81
    Willard Jehial (65) 82
Taylor, Margáret 42, 64
Ten Broke. Court of 24
Terhune, Jan Alberte 61
    Wilmin2 94
Ter Neirssan Court of 57

Thomassen, Capt. Wilhelm 58
Tillapaugh, Elizabeth Mae 130
Tobey, S. Elizabeth 127
Tomlinson, Harriet 83
    Jane Leslie 83
    John H. 83
Town, Simon 45, 48
Townsend, Elizabeth Abigail 104
    Joseph R. 104
Turner, Anna Nellie (265) 124
    Edmund Harvey 123
    Ellen May (266) 124
    Hattie Betsey (264) 124
    Nellie Schenck (152) 99, 123
    Samuel 123
Tyler, Emma R. 87
Tyson, Peter 38
Upson, Miles 50
van Arendahl, Aleid 56
van Bellinghoven, Aleid 24, 55
van Berlaer, Anna 57, 58
van Brempt, Engelbert 56
van Buren, Adelheit 56, 57
    Johann 56
van Couwenhoven, Albert Willemse 62
    Cornelius Willemse 36, 38, 62
    Garret Wolphertson 61
    Jacamyntie 40, 64
    Jacob 28
    Jacob Willemse 62
    Neeltje Geretsen 28, 61, 62
    Sara Willemse 36, 62
van Deventer, Peter 38
van Doren, Abram 45
    Jacob 38
    William 51
van Druse, Renad 22

van Egmont, Duke Carl 25
van Eyll, Elbricht 23
van Galen, Maria 57
van Huls, Frederick 56
 Lady Catherine 25
van Hochsteden, Conrad 22
van Julich, Count 16, 21, 23
van Kaldenbrock, Alheid 56
van Kelser, Marschall 22
van Mater, Joseph 63
van Oest, Isabella 56
van Rayde, Aleid 23, 55, 56
van Scherpenzeel, Johanna 58
van Schonan, Inugard 56
van Slyck, Anna 111
van Toutenburg, Barons of 21
van Voorhees, Coert 36
 Elizabeth Minnen 61
 Janetye 61
 Jan Lucase 62
 Neeltje Coerton 61
van der Donck, Adrian 28
van der Dussen, Jonkheer 6, 17, 55
van der Lippe, Caspar 27, 28
 Diderick 25, 26
Vanderveer, Agnes Mary 107
 Ann 79
 Catharine M. 52, 78
 Ella Bratt (85) 85, 107
 Garret 52, 79, 107
 Garret L. 107
 Hattie May (190) 107, 129
 Henry 107
 Henry (191) 107
 John Pomyea (192) 108
Vedder, Aaron F. 51, 83, 91
 Clyde Byron (125) 94

Vedder, Francis P. 94
    Frederick Fenner (119) 94, 116
    George Barry (123) 94
    George Sidney (234) 116
    Harriet Elnora (71) 83, 102
    Harriet Schenck (25) 67, 83
    Herbert Edward (236) 117
    Inez Ann (70) 83, 101
    James S. 51, 83, 94
    Jennie Leslie (73) 83
    Lyman Norton (72) 83, 103
    Nancy 83, 91
    Neil Davis (124) 94, 117
    Nichols (120) 94
    Ross Sylvester (122) 94, 116
    Sarah Fenner (46) 75, 93
    Sylvester A. 94
    Virginia Vertrees (233) 116
    Wilmina Wycoff (121) 94, 116
Verity, Eunice 80
    James G. 80
    Mary Ann 80
Vertrees, Cornelia Edna 116
    John 116
Vickery's Corners, N. Y. 45
Vincent, Adele Pauline (183) 104
    Eddie A. 104
    Nellie Smith (76) 84, 104
    Reuben 104
Voorhees, Henry Austin (167) 101
    Henry Peter (69) 82, 101
    James Hubbel (68) 82
    James L. 82
    James Leslie 45, 48, 82, 83, 86
    James Leslie 2nd (93) 86
    James Leslie 3rd (96) 86
    John Schenck (67) 82, 101

Voorhees, Leslie Eleanora (91) 86
    Margaret (94) 86
    Martha 82
    Martha (95) 86
    Martha Northrup (66) 82
    Parna Schenck (24) 48, 67, 82
    Peter 45, 48
    Sarah Bratt (34) 48, 70, 82, 86
    Sophia (92) 86
Wachtendonk, Feoffer of 23, 24, 55, 56
Walbeck, Castle of 23, 24, 55, 56
Walbrick, Heiress of 55
Wall, Betsey E. 119
Washburn, Zilpha 97
Watkins, Eunice M. 121
Weller, Melissa Almira 99
Wells, Charlotte Wilson (15) 66, 67, 81
    Eveline 101
    James F. 101
    Lillian B. 101
    Samuel 81
West, Samuel B. 44
Wilson, Ada Mary (162) 100, 126
    Alfred 47, 66, 85
    Austin Wycoff (14) 66, 80
    Charlotte M. (15) 66, 67, 81
Wilson's Corners, N. Y. 44
Wilson, Dennis Kennedy (16) 66, 81
    Eberle 116
    Eberle Irving (235) 116
    Francis A. (22) 67
    George W. 106
    Hannah 85
    James Alfred (20) 67
    Jane Ann (17) 66, 67, 81, 98
    John Cowan 116
    Louisa A. (19) 66, 82

Wilson, Lulu May 106

    Mary 66

    Matilda 85

    Mervin James (62) 80, 100

    Orinda M. (18) 66

    Orinda More (63) 81, 100

    Sally Schenck (2) 47, 65, 66, 85

    William 44, 47, 48, 66

    William 2nd 85

    William H. (21) 67

    Wilmina Vedder (121) 94, 116

Winchel, Sarah C. 84

Witherbee, Kathleen 116

    Thomas F. 116

Wolcott, John 130

    Nellie Mae 130

Wood, Jane 122

Wormuth, Charlotte 98

    Ella Lucretia 98

    Solomon 98

Wright, Charles 124

    Nellie 124

Wyckoff, Anetje Pieterse 30, 62

    John 38

    Peter 36

Benjamin Freeman Schenck, no 30

CPSIA information can be obtained
at www.ICGtesting.com
Printed in the USA
LVHW021953240323
742530LV00025B/558